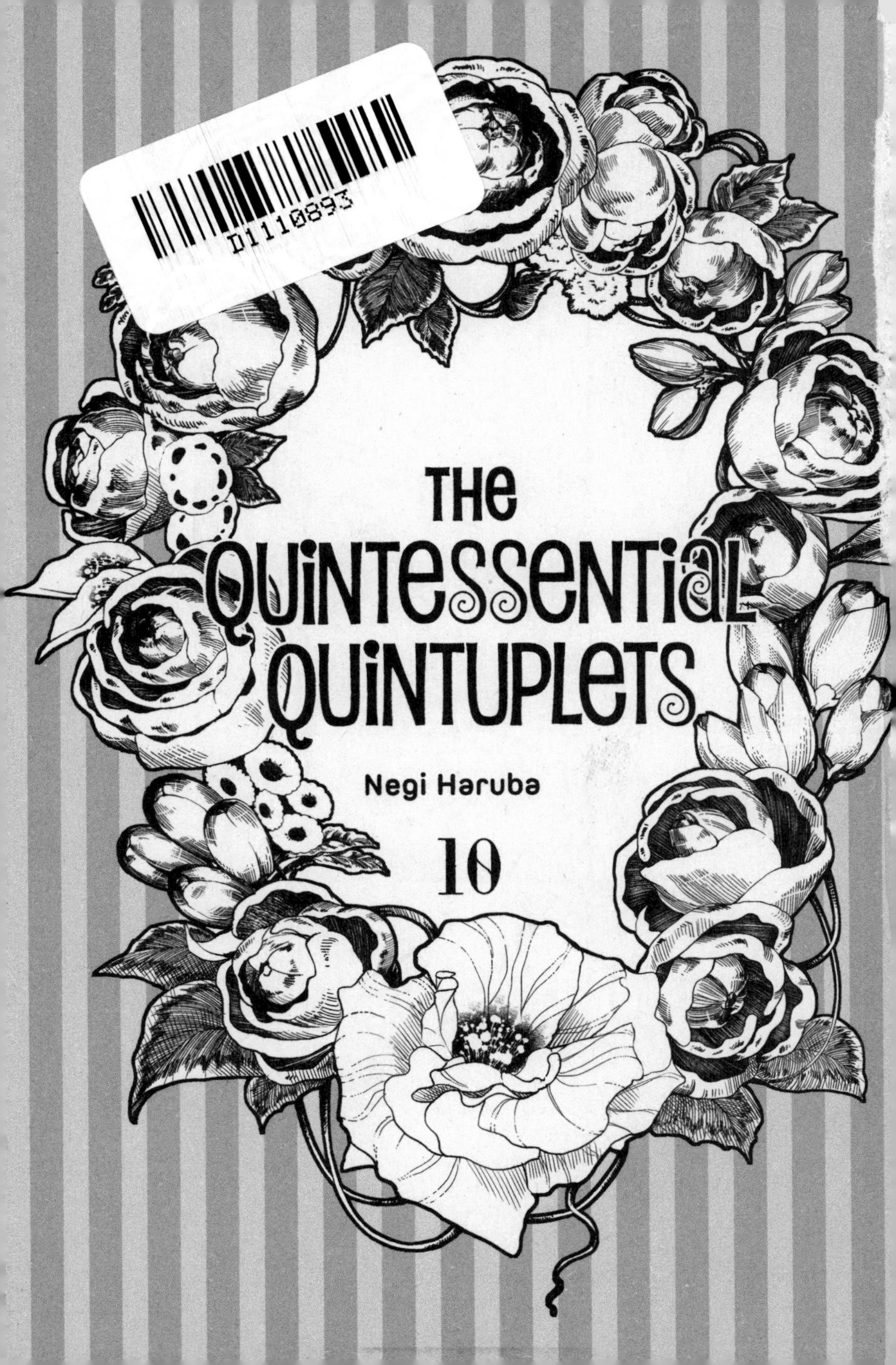

THE QUINTESSENTIAL QUINTUPLETS

Negi Haruba

10

Character intros
HIS FUTURE BRIDE IS ONE OF THE QUINTS!!
NINO NAKANO
THE SECOND SISTER. SHE'LL STAND IN LINE AS LONG AS IT TAKES TO GET HER TAPIOCA DRINK. HER FAVORITE PLACE IS HER PART-TIME JOB.
ICHIKA NAKANO
THE ELDEST SISTER. SHE'S REALLY BEEN ACTING LIKE THE ELDEST SISTER LATELY. HER FAVORITE PLACE IS BED.
Quints Memo
Hate to Study: If you try to teach them anything, they run.
Potential Flunkers: Their score on Futaro's quiz was 100 points...between the five of them.
On the Verge of Flunking: Had to change schools to avoid flunking out.
Very Idiosyncratic: The five sisters each have their own intense quirks, so dealing with them won't be easy.
...Guide the five of them to graduation!!

MIKU NAKANO
THE THIRD SISTER.
IT'S GOTTEN HOT OUT, BUT SHE KEEPS WEARING TIGHTS THROUGH PURE DETERMINATION. HER FAVORITE PLACE IS THE GAP BETWEEN THINGS.
YOTSUBA NAKANO
THE FOURTH SISTER.
THE BODY OF AN ADULT BUT THE MIND OF A CHILD. ALSO, THE UNDERWEAR OF A CHILD. HER FAVORITE PLACE IS ON A SWING SET.
ITSUKI NAKANO
THE FIFTH SISTER.
WHEN SHE HEARS PEOPLE TALKING ABOUT THE "MAY BLUES," SHE GETS KIND OF DEPRESSED. HER FAVORITE PLACE IS THE PET SHOP.

FUTARO UESUGI
ONE BARBECUE MEAL.
MINUS THE BARBECUE.
THE QUINTUPLETS' PRIVATE TUTOR. HAS BEEN TRAGICALLY CAUGHT UP IN A WAR WITHOUT EVEN KNOWING IT. HIS FAVORITE PLACE IS HIS DESK.

NOW WE'LL ACTUALLY BE ABLE TO FILL OUR BELLIES, HUH, BIG BROTHER?
RAIHA UESUGI
FUTARO'S SISTER. ELDEST DAUGHTER. HER FAVORITE PLACE IS THE ARCADE.

CONTENTS

CRONCH

CHAPTER 78
SISTERS' WAR: ROUND 1

UM... THIS IS A BAKERY, ISN'T IT, MIKU?
NOT SOME KIND OF ROCK STORE...

...

W-WELL, NAKANO-SAN ONLY STARTED RECENTLY...

BAKING IS DIFFICULT. EVERYONE STARTS OUT LIKE THIS.
LUCKILY WE'RE NOT AS INTIMIDATING AS THE BAKERY ACROSS THE STREET.

こむぎや
KOMUGIYA
I'LL TEACH YOU AS MUCH AS I CAN, SO JUST FOCUS ON IMPROVING!
YES, MA'AM!

OOZE

IT'S KIND OF GOOEY...
IT'S SO WEIRD... I HAVE HER FOLLOW THE PROPER PROCEDURE, BUT SOME STRANGE POWER AL-WAYS MAKES HER FAIL.
AND THAT SHOP ACROSS THE WAY'S BEEN DOING WELL LATELY...
MAYBE I'M NOT CUT OUT FOR BAKING...
H-HAVE SOME CONFI-DENCE!

こむぎや
KOMUGIYA
I THINK IT'S CLOSER TO FOOD THIS TIME!
YOU'RE ON THE RIGHT TRACK!
OKAY...

BURNT

IT'S BREAD...
THAT BREAD I ATE THE OTHER DAY WASN'T JUST A HALLUCINATION!

WE STILL CAN'T SERVE IT TO CUSTOMERS...

...BUT I'M GLAD YOU'VE MANAGED TO IMPROVE THIS MUCH, MIKU-CHAN...

THANK YOU, BOSS.
LET'S GO HAVE UESUGI-SAN TRY IT! HE WON'T BELIEVE IT!
IT MAY BE BREAD, BUT IT'S STILL NOT DELICIOUS BREAD.
DIDN'T YOU SAY YOU WANTED IT TO BE READY BEFORE YOUR FIELD TRIP, MIKU-CHAN?
YES.
WE'RE SUPPOSED TO BE FREE TO EAT WHATEVER WE LIKE FOR LUNCH ON THE FIRST DAY...

THAT'S WHEN I'LL GIVE HIM MY SECRET WEAPON,
WITH AN ATTACK AS SWIFT AS FLAMES.

OH YEAH?
I'M SURE HE'LL LOVE IT!

BUT THERE'S ONE OTHER PROB-LEM...
?

NOW THAT WE HAVE COMPLETED THE NATION-AL MOCK EXAM...

...I WOULD LIKE TO BEGIN SERIOUSLY DISCUSSING THE FIELD TRIP.

3 - 1

Field Trip
THE BASIC SCHEDULE FOR THE THREE DAYS IS INCLUDED IN THE PAMPHLETS ALREADY GIVEN OUT.

SO WE ASK THAT YOU ALL SELECT YOUR GROUPS BY TOMORROW.
MURMUR
MURMUR
MURMUR

MURMUR
DURING THE TRIP, YOU WILL DO ALL OF YOUR ACTIVITIES WITH THIS GROUP.
MURMUR
MURMUR
AND GROUPS CAN CONTAIN UP TO FIVE MEMBERS.
MURMUR
MURMUR
MURMUR
...

IF WE AREN'T IN THE SAME GROUP, WE MAY NOT BE ABLE TO EAT TOGETHER.

BUT I MOSTLY WANT TO SEE KYOTO WITH HIM.

LEAVE IT TO ME,
MIKU!

YOU AND ME SHOULD FORM A GROUP WITH UESUGI-SAN!
I'LL TELL HIM!
HUH?! ARE YOU SURE?
DING
DONG
LET'S SEE... UESUGI-SAN... UESUGI-SAN...

THERE HE IS!
HEY, UESUGI-S—
YOTSU-BA.
!
COME HERE A SECOND.
WHAT IS IT, ICHIKA?

I CAN'T WAIT FOR THE FIELD TRIP. CAN YOU?
THIS WILL BE OUR FIRST TIME TOGETHER IN KYOTO, RIGHT?
NO WAY! WE WENT IN ELEMENTARY SCHOOL, REMEMBER?
OH, THAT'S RIGHT.
IS THERE ANYWHERE YOU'D LIKE TO VISIT, YOTSUBA?
LIKE EVERYONE, JUST THE TEMPLES, I GUESS?
I THINK THE REST OF THE CLASS IS HAVING TROUBLE MAKING GROUPS OF FIVE, BUT THAT'S PERFECT FOR US, ISN'T IT?
OH! HAHA...
LUCKY WE'RE QUINTUPLETS, HUH?

BUT I WONDER WHAT FUTARO-KUN'S GOING TO DO.

HE'S A THIRD-YEAR, BUT I STILL DON'T THINK HE HAS ANY FRIENDS.
BIG SISTER'S WORRIED ABOUT HIM.

UHHH...
IN THAT CASE...

OH WELL.
I GUESS WE'LL HAVE TO DO SOMETHING ABOUT IT.

HUH?
ICHIKA?

A GROUP OF YOU, ME, AND FUTARO-KUN.
THAT'S GOOD WITH YOU, RIGHT?
!
OH, SORRY. I'VE GOT A PHONE CALL.
YOU HANDLE IT, YOTSUBA.
HUH?! WAIT A...
...

図書室
NOW WHAT'M I GONNA DO...?

Library

OH.
MIKU'S ACTUALLY HERE TODAY.
I'VE GOT WORK LATER, BUT I'LL STAY FOR A BIT.
THIS IS THE FIRST TIME WE'VE ALL BEEN HERE AT ONCE SINCE THE NATIONAL MOCK EXAM.
OH YEAH, I GUESS IT'S BEEN A WEEK SINCE THEN, HUH?

WHAT'S WITH THE PASSIONATE GAZE?
HUH?! WHATEVER DO YOU MEAN?!
LET US HIT THE BOOKS! QUICKLY!
FIRST...

I WANT TO TALK ABOUT THE FIELD TRIP.
HUH?
!

FUTARO, HAVE YOU DECIDED WHO YOU'RE GOING TO GROUP WITH?
!
WAIT!
I'M-

YOTSUBA HAS SOME-THING TO TELL YOU!
WHUMP
HUH?!

U-
UM...

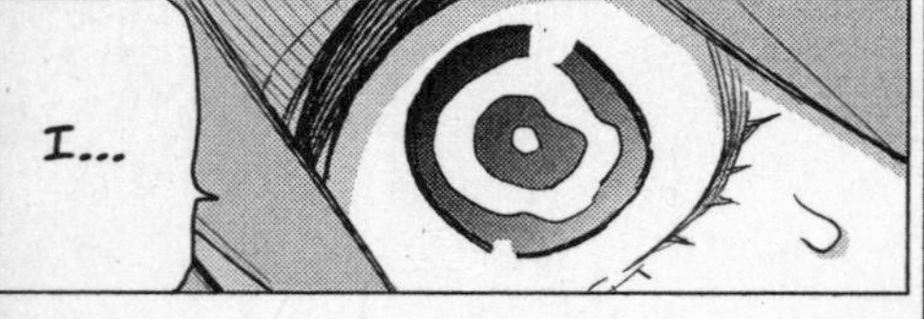
I...

GO ON.
SAY IT.
WHAT IS IT?
SPIT IT OUT ALREADY.

SO, UM...
ME AND MIKU AND ICHIKA WANT TO...
BUT WHAT ABOUT ITSUKI AND NINO? SISTERS SHOULD STICK TOGETHER...
OH, I KNOW!

WHY DON'T WE ALL MAKE ONE BIG GROUP?!
WITH UESUGI-SAN, TOO!
HUH?
THAT WOULD BE THE BEST SOLUTION, BUT...
FIVE MEMBERS IS THE LIMIT...
YEAH.

I MEAN EVERYONE BUT ME! I'LL JOIN A DIFFERENT GROUP!
THAT SOLVES EVERYTHING, RIGHT?

I THINK THAT'S GOING A LITTLE FAR...

YOTSUBA, I CAN'T DO THAT.
HUH?

IS THERE A PROBLEM?
...
YEAH... A BIG PROB-LEM...
YES.

NO ONE WANTS THAT.
AT LEAST, I DON'T.

WHAT ABOUT THIS?

FU-KUN AND I WILL BE OUR OWN GROUP OF TWO.
!
FU-KUN?
I DON'T KNOW WHAT YOTSUBA WAS GOING TO PROPOSE...
...BUT THIS WAS MY PLAN FROM THE VERY BEGINNING.

I'LL SEE THE SIGHTS WITH THE BOY I LOVE.
AND I WON'T TAKE NO FOR AN ANSWER.

THEN WHAT UESUGI-KUN SAID WAS TRUE...
WHICH MEANS... DON'T TELL ME...

ICHIKA REALLY DOES LIKE HIM, TOO?
SHE GOT ME!
WHEN SHE DECLARES IT IN FRONT OF EVERYONE LIKE THAT, THERE'S NOTHING I CAN DO.
H-HEY...
NINO, YOU CAN'T JUST DECIDE-
YOU STAY OUT OF THIS, FU-KUN!
FU-KUN...

M-
ME TOO...

IF YOU HAVE SOMETHING TO SAY...
...THEN GO AHEAD...
...AND SAY IT RIGHT NOW.

THAT SETTLES IT.
DON'T SETTLE IT.

LISTEN TO ME!
I TOLD YOU TO STAY OUT OF THIS!

YOU JUST BE GRATEFUL FOR THE FACT THAT YOU GET TO GO ON A DATE WITH ME! GOT IT?!

I ALREADY JOINED A GROUP WITH SOME GUYS FROM CLASS.
SORRY.

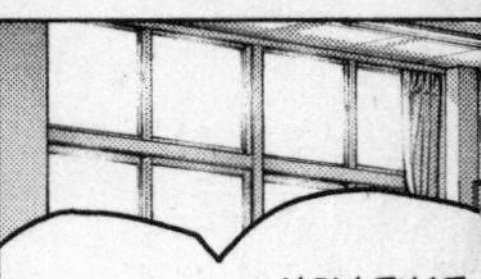
NOW THAT YOU HAVE FINISHED DIVIDING INTO GROUPS...
...PLEASE REMEMBER TO SELECT A GROUP LEADER.

SO WHO'S GONNA BE OUR LEADER? HUH?
WHO ELSE BUT ME?
I FORGOT YOU'RE IN CLASS ONE TOO...

WHY DID IT TURN OUT LIKE THIS?

I FIGURED THOSE FIVE WOULD END UP IN A GROUP.
AND I WAS... HOPING TO GET INTO THE SAME GROUP AS ICHIKA-SAN!
BUT THEY MUST GET ALONG PRETTY WELL IF ALL THE SISTERS FORMED A GROUP.

THE SAME AS ALWAYS...
HAHA...
WELL, I'M GLAD FUTARO-KUN MADE SOME FRIENDS...

...

THIS IS SO AWKWARD!

CHAPTER 79
SISTERS' WAR: ROUND 2

UESUGI-KUN...

CHACK
HUH? IT'S JUST YOU, ITSUKI?
Y-YES!

HMM? DID YOU JUST PUT SOMETHING IN YOUR BAG?
YES!
I WAS JUST PREPARING FOR THE TRIP.

OH.
IT *IS* PRETTY SOON, HUH?

...
THINGS HAVE BEEN KIND OF WEIRD BETWEEN US LATELY...

I HOPE EVERYONE CAN MAKE UP DURING THE FIELD TRIP!

AGREED.
I BELIEVE WE CAN RETURN TO THE WAY WE WERE BEFORE.

ALL RIGHT! I THINK I'LL START PACKING, TOO!
WHAT DO WE NEED AGAIN?
AREN'T YOU SUP-POSED TO BRING...
...UNDER-WEAR, SOCKS, AND A TOOTH-BRUSH?
MEN'S SOCKS
2F

HEY, DOES ALL THAT REALLY HAVE TO BE NEW, RAIHA?
WHAT? BUT YOUR UNDER-WEAR'S FALLING APART, BIG BROTHER.
EVERYONE WILL LAUGH AT YOU!
PEOPLE ARE LAUGHING AT ME RIGHT NOW.
HEH
HEH
Statio nery

YOU'RE OFFICIALLY BACK AS THE QUINTS' TUTOR, SO THERE'S NOTHING WRONG WITH SPENDING A LITTLE MONEY ON YOURSELF.
OH, BUT...
...THE QUINTUPLETS WON'T LIKE IT IF YOU SKIMP ON THEIR BIRTHDAY PRESENTS.
HUH, THEIR BIRTHDAY'S COMING UP?

HUH?!
IT ALREADY HAPPENED.
WELL... IT'S NO BIG DEAL IF I DON'T GET THEM ANY-THING...
THEY WERE LATE WITH MINE, AFTER ALL...
PLUS, IF THEY DIDN'T SAY ANYTHING ABOUT IT...
UUUGH...
IF YOU GET SOME-THING, YOU GIVE SOME-THING IN RETURN!
EVEN ELEMENTARY SCHOOLERS KNOW THAT!

TMP
TMP
TMP
!
SO, SHOULD I GET YOU SOMETHING?
EEK!

OH!
OF ALL THE PEOPLE TO RUN INTO...
UESUGI-SAN!
AND HEY THERE, RAIHA-CHAN!

I TEXTED ITSUKI-SAN YESTERDAY.
I THOUGHT WE COULD GO SHOP-PING TOGETHER.
OH YEAH? LOOK, ABOUT YOUR BIRTHDAY-

I SHOULD HAVE ASSUMED YOU WOULD BE COMING WITH HER...
IN THAT CASE, WE CANNOT SHOP TOGETH-ER.

AHHH! SHHH! SHHH!

OOF!

YOU'RE SMART, BIG BROTHER, SO CAN'T YOU THINK OF SOMETHING YOURSELF?

?

IF I OBSERVE WHAT THEY BUY, I MIGHT LEARN WHAT KIND OF GIFTS THEY'D WANT...
WH-WHY ARE YOU FOLLOWING ME?!
WE'RE PROBABLY BUYING THE SAME THINGS, RIGHT? WHAT'S THE PROBLEM?
YES, THAT'S RIGHT!
BUT EVEN IF THEY ARE THE SAME ITEMS, THEY ARE VERY DIFFER-ENT...
WHAT?
WE'RE HERE! TO BUY UNDERWEAR!
DÉJÁ VU!!

ITSUKI-SAN! I THINK THIS IS A LITTLE TOO MATURE!
I-I-I-I AM IN HIGH SCHOOL! THIS IS NORMAL!

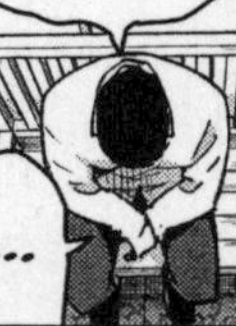

BUT SHE'S GOT HER EXCEPTION-AL PHYSICAL ABILITIES.

IF WE LOOK AT SOMETHING IN THAT FIELD, WE SHOULD BE ABLE TO FIND SOMETHING SHE'S SUITED FOR.

ALL
SMILE
SORRY FOR THE WAIT!
HUH? WHERE'S ITSUKI?
SHE'S BEING MEA-SURED AND TRYING THINGS ON IN BACK.
YOU'RE QUINTUPLETS, SO CAN'T SHE JUST GET THE SAME SIZE AS THE REST OF YOU?
TWEET
TWEET
AH! THAT'S QUIN-TUPLET HARASS-MENT!
QUIN-TASS-MENT!
...
BUT IT IS WEIRD SHE'S GETTING NEW MEA-SUREMENTS TAKEN...
GASP!
COULD ITSUKI BE PULLING OUT AHEAD...?
IT MUST BE TOUGH BEING QUINTU-PLETS.
THAT'S RIGHT. I MEAN, JUST LATELY...
?
N-
NO, NEVER MIND!
ANYWAY! THE CAMPING TRIP KIND OF ENDED ON A BAD NOTE...
SO THIS TIME!

WHUMP

LET'S MAKE THIS A FIELD TRIP YOU WON'T REGRET!
BEEEAAAAM

I DON'T CARE ONE WAY OR THE OTHER.
BUT I'LL TRY TO WATCH MY HEALTH THIS TIME.
JEEZ, I KNOW YOU'RE LOOKING FORWARD TO IT!

YOU KEEP RE-READING THE GUIDE BOOK AT HOME!
RAIHA!!
AND...

...YOU MIGHT RUN INTO THE GIRL FROM THAT PICTURE, TOO.

WHAT? NOT LIKELY...
HUH? BUT DIDN'T DAD SAY YOU MET HER IN KYOTO?
YEAH, BUT SHE WAS ON A TRIP, TOO...
THE GIRL FROM THAT PICTURE? WHAT DO YOU MEAN?
...
WHIRL
くるくる
WHIRL
GO ON, SHOW HER!
IT'S NOTHING.
I DON'T EVEN HAVE THE PICTURE ANYMORE.
GRR!

YOU'RE ACTING REALLY FISHY!
IF IT'S NOTHING, THEN YOU SHOULD BE ABLE TO TELL ME!
BUT I CAN TELL WHY YOU WON'T!
BECAUSE YOU CAN'T FORGET HER!

GO AHEAD AND TELL ME! YOU'LL FEEL BETTER GETTING IT OFF YOUR CHEST!
WOW, SHE'S ACTUALLY OVERPOWERING BIG BROTHER...
HE WEAKENS A LOT WHEN THE TOPIC TURNS TO THIS SORT OF THING.

SHE'S A GIRL I RAN INTO IN KYOTO.
HER NAME'S RENA.
HUH?!
RENA...?
THE END.
THE END?!
I-I REALLY WANT TO HEAR MORE...
COULD YOU GIVE ME A FEW MORE DETAILS?
LONG STORY SHORT, SHE WAS HIS FIRST LOVE!
HUH?!
HIS...
HIS FIRST LOVE?!

HEY... WHO SAID SHE WAS MY FIRST-

EH HEH HEH, TALKING ABOUT FOOD MADE ME HUNGRY!
NO ONE SAID A WORD ABOUT FOOD...
TH- THEN...
...I'LL BUY YOU WHATEVER YOU WANT!

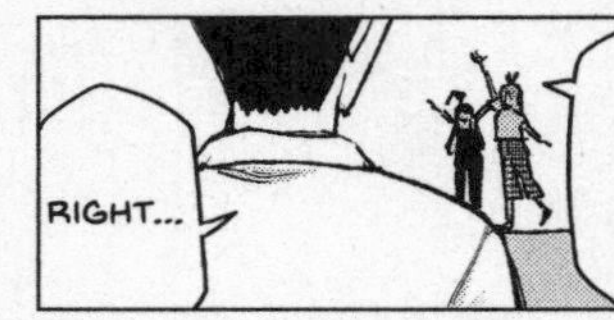

YOU'RE IN CHARGE OF WAITING FOR ITSUKI, UESUGI-SAN!
RIGHT...

I'M BEAT...

YOU'RE NOT SURPRISING ME THIS TIME...

RENA.
OH?
THAT'S TOO BAD.

I HEAR YOU'RE GOING TO KYOTO FOR A FIELD TRIP.
DOESN'T THAT TAKE YOU BACK?
I THOUGHT YOU WEREN'T GOING TO SHOW YOURSELF ANYMORE.
WHY DID YOU SHOW UP AGAIN?

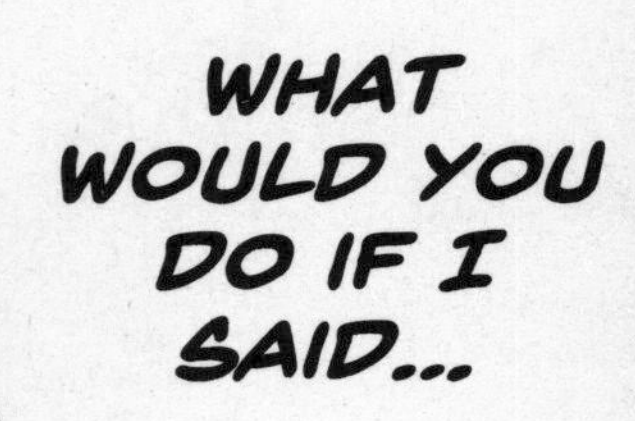
WHAT WOULD YOU DO IF I SAID...

...IT WAS BECAUSE I WANTED TO SEE YOU?

DON'T WE SEE EACH OTHER ALL THE TIME?

HUH?

HUH?!
RENA.

WHY DID YOU USE YOUR MOTHER'S NAME?

HAHA...
SO YOU'VE ALREADY FIGURED OUT THAT MUCH...

BACK THEN, IT WAS JUST A SPUR OF THE MOMENT THING...
I'M GLAD YOU SAID THAT THOUGH. THAT'S WHAT I WANTED TO TELL YOU...
...BUT I WAS CONCERNED YOU WOULDN'T BELIEVE ME...

JUST AS YOU SUS-PECT...
...I AM ONE OF THE QUINTU-PLETS.
CAN YOU TELL WHO I AM?

NO!
SO JUST TELL ME!
DOESN'T FLAT-OUT ASKING ME TAKE ALL THE FUN OUT OF IT?
YOU'VE GOT GREAT GRADES, SO USE YOUR BRAIN A LITTLE!
I'M TIRED OF WORRYING ABOUT...
..WHO'S WHO... AND WHO'S ACTING LIKE WHOM.

YOU GAVE UP TOO EASILY!

DON'T RAIN ON MY FIELD TRIP PARADE.
SHOO! SHOO!

D- DON'T YOU WANT TO KNOW?
DON'T YOU...
...CARE ABOUT ME ANYMORE?
YOU'RE-
WHUMP
...
OH! THE CUS-TOMER WHO WAS USING THIS FITTING ROOM...
I FOUND HER BAG, BUT THAT'S ALL.
I'M SORRY.
SHACK

NOTHING'S GOING HOW I WANT...
BUT...
...I'VE LAID THE GROUND-WORK.
新大阪・博多方面
ひかり 495 7:37 広
こだま 695 7:56 新大
りぞみ 5 8:13 博
りぞみ 201 8:24 新大
IT'S FINALLY ABOUT TO BEGIN!
HEY, ITSUKI!
LET'S BOARD THE BULLET TRAIN!

FIRST, LET'S FOLLOW FU-KUN'S GROUP.
NOD NOD
FUTARO-KUN DIDN'T SEEM THRILLED ABOUT THAT...
STOP CALLING HIM "FU-KUN."
UESUGI-KUN!

LET'S GO TO KIYOMIZU-DERA!
YOUR GROUP AND OURS!
HUH?
WAIT, AREN'T GROUPS SUPPOSED TO MOVE INDEPENDENTLY?
!
OH, DON'T BE LIKE THAT.
I THOUGHT YOUR MEMORIES OF KYOTO WERE IMPORTANT TO YOU?
I HAVE FAITH THAT YOU WILL NOTICE.

HUH?!
WHY IS ITSUKI...
NOW ITSUKI'S ACTING FUNNY, TOO?!

CHAPTER 80
SISTERS' WAR: ROUND 3

FWOOOS
WHERE'S YOUR GROUP GOING?
WE'RE ALL GOING TO TEMPLES AND SHRINES ON THE SECOND DAY, RIGHT?
SO I WAN-NA HAVE ALL KINDS OF FUN ON THE FIRST DAY!
I KNOW, RIGHT?
THERE, FULL HOUSE.
HRNGH...
I LOSE~...

ONE MOR ONE MOR HAND!
I'LL TAKE YOU ON ANYTIME.

MIKU.
MIKU!

DAZED...
IT'S OVER.
NOD
NOD
!

OH.
TWO PAIRS.
YOU'RE LATE! AND YOUR HAND'S WEAK!

YOU SEEM SLEEPY.
YOU WOKE UP EARLY THIS MORNING AND WENT OFF SOME-WHERE, DIDN'T YOU?
WHISPER
WHISPER
YEAH.

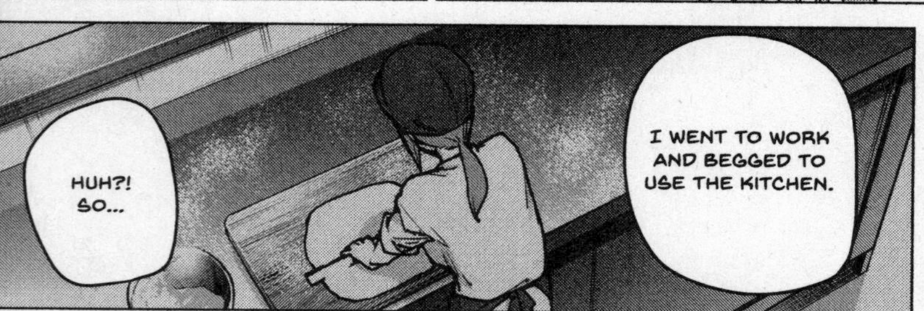
I WENT TO WORK AND BEGGED TO USE THE KITCHEN.
HUH?! SO...

...YOU'RE FINALLY GOING TO HAVE HIM TASTE IT AND THEN TELL HIM?
WHOOM
WHOOM

YOU'VE BEEN WORKING YOUR BUTT OFF FOR THIS DAY!
I'LL BE CHEERING FOR YOU TILL THE VERY END.

I HOPE IT'S STILL GOOD COLD...

I KNO
HOW ABOUT FOR THIS NEXT HAND WE MAKE A RULE...
...THAT THE WINNER GETS TO GIVE ANY ORDER THEY LIKE?
ANY ORDER?
GOOD IDEA.
I ACCEPT.
I WON'T LOSE.

メラメラメラ
FWOOM
メラメラメラ
FWOOM

THESE SPARKS ARE FLYING...
...BECAUSE THEY'RE SO FIRED UP ABOUT CARDS, RIGHT?!
HOOONK

WE WILL SEND THE LARGE ITEMS TO THE HOTEL OURSELVES.
ONLY TAKE YOUR VALUABLES WITH YOU.

THOSE ARE ALL THE TIPS WE HAVE.

DISMISSED.
SNAP

IS SOMETHING THE MATTER?
HUH? NO.
IT WAS PROBABLY JUST MY IMAGINA-TION.

I WONDER WHERE FU-KUN'S GROUP IS GOING...
WHERE DOES EVERYONE WANNA GO?

WELL, WE ARE ON A TRIP...AND TRIPS MEAN SHOPPING!
FANCY SHOPS ARE A LOT MORE FUN THAN MOLDY OLD TEMPLES!

YOU DON'T GET IT, DO YOU? THIS IS KYOTO.
SO I WANT TO FEED HIM ALL THE DELICIOUS LOCAL TREATS.

I AGREE WITH THAT OPINION, BUT...
...AT THE MOMENT, I'D LIKE TO REMIND HIM OF WHAT HAPPENED THAT DAY... NO, I MEAN, UM, A WALK WOULD BE NICE...

ITSUKI?
WHAT'S GOTTEN INTO YOU ALL OF A SUDDEN?

I—
AH!
FUTARO-KUN'S GROUP JUST LEFT!

IF THEY WON'T JUST JOIN UP WITH HIS GROUP...
...THEN WE MUST ALL BE THINKING THE SAME THING...
LET'S FOLLOW THEM...

I WONDER WHERE THEY'RE GOING...

CLAP
CLAP

WHAT IS THIS PLACE?
A SHRINE TO THE GOD OF ACADEMICS.
MAEDA-KUN, YOUR GRADES ARE HARD TO LOOK AT, SO PRAY DEEPLY.
...

THE HELL DID YOU SAY?
SHUT UP, YOU TWO!
IT'S PRETTY PLAIN, ISN'T IT?
NOW, NOW.

LOOKS LIKE THEY'RE MOVING ON.
I THINK THERE'S A SHRINE NEXT DOOR, TOO.

AND THIS IS THE ONLY DAY WE'RE FREE TO EAT WHAT WE LIKE...
THIS WHOLE GROUP BUSINES IS MY GREATES OBSTACLE...

IT'S OKAY!
I'M SURE YOU'LL HAVE A CHANCE TO TALK TO HIM ALONE!

WOW!
DO THESE GATES JUST KEEP GOING?!

I'VE SEEN THEM IN PHOTOGRAPHS...
...BUT THEY'RE QUITE MAGNIFICENT IN PERSON.
WHAT A SHOT~!
COME ON.
FLASH THOSE PEACE SIGNS, GIRLS.
ONES WITH JUST US SISTERS ARE PRETTY IMPORTANT TOO, HUH?

OH, WE DON'T HAVE ANY OF JUST THE FIVE OF US?
WE DIDN'T TAKE ONE OF US AT THE FIREWORKS FESTIVAL?
WE HAVEN'T TAKEN ONE SINCE WE WERE ON OUR FIELD TRIP BACK IN ELEMENTARY SCHOOL.
THEN LET'S TAKE ONE WITH EVERYONE...
DO YOU THINK FUTARO'S ALREADY UP TOP?
I DON'T SEE HIM.
BOYS MOVE FAST.
ALL RIGHT!
THEN LET'S GO ALL OUT TOO!

HUFF...
HUFF...

THIS STAIR-WAY'S...
...PRETTY LONG... HUH?
MY LEGS ARE STARTING TO HURT...
SHEESH, YOU'RE ALL SO SLOW!

I'M GLAD SOMEONE DOESN'T HAVE A CARE IN THE WORLD.
THAT'S YOTSUBA'S STRENGTH
I KNOW.
SHE'S A LOT DIFFERENT FROM A CERTAIN SCHEMER I KNOW.
!

I'M SURE YOU'VE GOT SOMETHING UP YOUR SLEEVE TODAY TOO, RIGHT?
HAHA...
NO...
NOT TODAY, ANYWAY.
CLENCH

四ツ辻
YOTSUTSUJI INTERSECTION

LOOKS LIKE THERE'S TWO PATHS.

AND THEY BOTH GO TO THE TOP OF THE MOUNTAIN.

I WONDER WHICH WAY FU-KUN WENT...
IF I DON'T RUN INTO HIM HERE, IT'LL BE A HUGE LOSS...

IT'S ALREADY NOON, SO WHY DON'T WE STOP THERE FOR LUNCH?
!

WAIT...
CAN'T WE HAVE LUNCH, UM...
...

WHAT?
YOU WANT TO EAT SOME-THING DIFFER-ENT?
UMMM...
...

FULL HOUSE.

LET'S SPLIT INTO TWO GROUPS!
HUH?

MIKU AND I WILL TAKE THE RIGHT ROUTE.

ICHIKA, NINO, AND ITSUKI WILL TAKE THE LEFT ONE.
THAT WAY WE'LL RUN INTO UESUGI-SAN FOR SURE!

WAIT A SECOND!
YOU CAN'T JUST GO DECIDING THAT ALONE...

I WON, SO WHAT I SAY GOES!
FWOOOSH
I WON THE RIGHT TO GIVE ANY ORDER I WANT!
UGH!

LEFT ROUTE

YOUR FUN LITTLE GAME CERTAINLY SCREWED THINGS UP.

JUDGING FROM THE FLOW OF THE CROWD, THE OTHER ROUTE IS THE NORMAL ONE.
THEY MIGHT BEAT US TO HIM.

UM...
WHAT ARE YOU GIRLS TALKING—

OH.

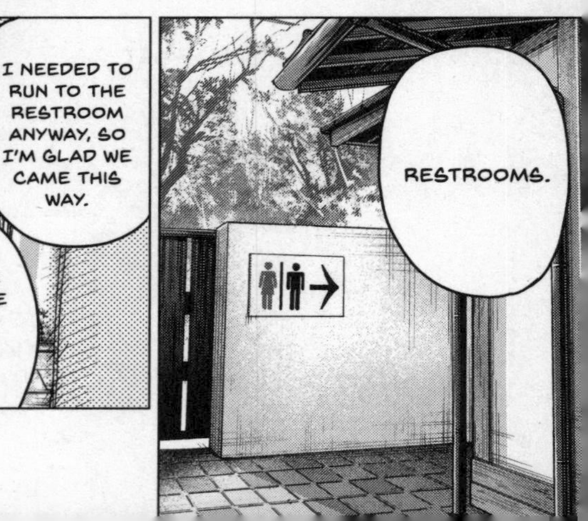
RESTROOMS.

I NEEDED TO RUN TO THE RESTROOM ANYWAY, SO I'M GLAD WE CAME THIS WAY.
I DOUBT THERE'LL BE ANOTHER ONE ON THE WAY, SO I'LL GO, TOO.

RIGHT ROUTE

MIKU~!
YOU'VE GOTTA HURRY OR LUNCH'LL BE OVER~!
YEAH... WE'RE ALMOST THERE...

YOU'VE BEEN WORKING SO HARD FOR THIS DAY.
JUST HANG IN THERE A LITTLE LONGER!
YOTSU-BA...
THANK YOU...

IT'S LUNCH-TIME... I'M FAMISHED...
I WONDER WHAT FU-KUN'S GROUP IS PLANNING TO DO FOR LUNCH?
HUH?

WHERE'S ICHIKA?

CRAP...

HUFF
HUFF

JUDGING FROM THE MAP, THIS ROUTE IS SHORTER.

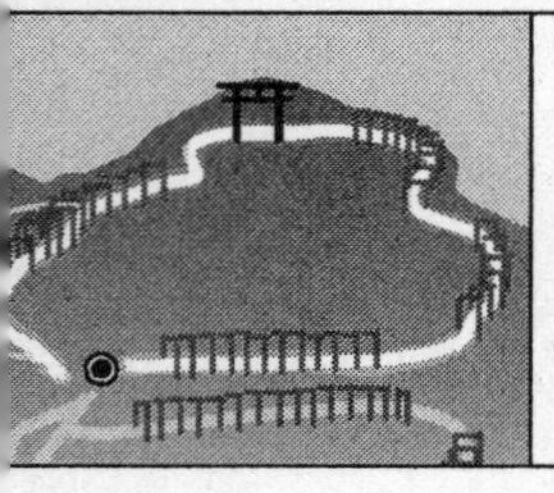

IF I WERE ONLY COMPETING WITH YOTSUBA, I MIGHT LOSE...

...BUT IF I TAKE INTO ACCOUNT MIKU'S LACK OF STAMINA, I SHOULD REACH THE TOP FIRST!

WHAT AM I GONNA DO WHEN I RUN INTO FUTARO-KUN?
AND THE REST OF HIS GROUP WILL BE THERE, TOO.
BUT MIKU'S ACTING ODD.
SHE'S DEFINITELY PLANNING TO MAKE A MOVE DURING THIS TRIP.
I'LL HAVE TO DO IT AGAIN.
I CAN'T TAKE BACK A LIE I'VE ALREADY TOLD, SO...

...IN ORDER TO STOP MIKU...
...I'LL KEEP LYING UNTIL THIS ROLE IS FINISHED.

14
MADE IT...
!

白菊大神
白菊大神
NO ONE'S HERE...

IF I DIDN'T RUN INTO THEM ON THE LEFT-HAND ROUTE...

...THEN FUTARO-KUN MUST STILL BE ON THE RIGHT-HAND ROUTE!

I'VE GOTTA HURRY!
TMP
TMP
I RAN THIS HARD, SO MIKU AND THE OTH-ERS MUST STILL-

...HUH?
BA-DUMP
BA-DUMP
BA-DUMP

ICHIKA...
WHY ARE YOU DISGUISED AS ME?

...

?
ICHI-KA?
IF YOU HAVE A REASON, THEN-
ICHIKA.

THIS ISN'T...
...WHAT I MEANT WHEN I SAID IT.
IS THAT REALLY WHAT YOU WANT TO DO?

YOTSUBA?
WHAT ARE YOU TALKING ABOUT?
ICHIKA'S TRYING TO GET IN THE WAY.
IN THE WAY OF WHAT?
CLACK
!
SHE'S TRYING TO-
YOTSUBA!
WAIT!

SHE'S TRYING TO STOP YOU FROM TELLING UESUGI-SAN YOU LIKE HIM!
ALL RIGHT! FIRST!
WHOOSH
HUMP
HUH?
WHAT...
...DID YOU JUST SAY?
GRIP

CHAPTER 81
SISTERS' WAR: ROUND 4
UESUGI-SAN...

YOU DIDN'T HEAR WHAT I JUST SAID, DID-
MIKU!
WHUMP
PHEW... WE FINALLY MADE IT.
!
MIKU?!
WAIT A SECOND, MIKU!
WHERE ARE YOU GOING?!

!
...
ICHIKA...
YOU REALLY DID IT, DIDN'T YOU?
STOP SCREWING AROUND!

NOW YOU'VE MADE HER CRY...
ARE YOU SATISFIED?

FWIP
WAIT, NINO.
THIS WAS MY-

IT'S ALL RIGHT, YOTSUBA.
NO MATTER THE RESULT...
...THIS IS MORE OR LESS WHAT I WAS TRYING TO DO.

HOW FAR WILL YOU GO TO-
I DON'T WANT TO HEAR THAT FROM YOU OF ALL PEOPLE, NINO.
REMEMBER WHAT YOU SAID IN THE HOT SPRING?
YOU SAID YOU'D DEFEAT WHOEVER IT TOOK TO MAKE YOUR LOVE COME TRUE.
WHAT'S THE DIFFERENCE BETWEEN YOU AND ME?
GO AHEAD. TELL ME.
YES, I DID SAY THAT.
AND I DON'T INTEND TO LET ANYONE HAVE HIM.
BUT...

...MY BOND WITH MY SISTERS...
...IS JUST AS IMPORT-ANT.

EVEN IF THE DAY CAME WHEN HE CHOSE YOU INSTEAD...
...I...
...I'D WANT TO BE HAPPY FOR YOU!
...!
URP! I CAN'T WALK ANOTHER STEP...
HONESTLY, YOU ATE TOO MUCH AT THE RESTAURANT BELOW.
HUH?
WHAT'S GOIN' ON HERE? HUH?!
DON'T ASK ME... I'VE GOT NO IDEA EITHER...
TMP
LOOK, GIRLS, WHY DON'T YOU BOTH SETTLE DOWN FOR A–
!

SHUT UP!
YOU STAY OUT OF THIS BEFORE THINGS GET EVEN MESSIER!
GO AFTER MIKU RIGHT NOW!
HUH?
HURRY! RUN!
...
ALL RIGHT...
MURMUR
SORRY, GUYS. I'VE GOTTA GO.
MURMUR MURMUR
RIGHT...
I-I'LL LOOK FOR HER, TOO!

WHAT THE? WAS THERE A FIGHT?
SOME STUDENTS ARE FIGHTING.
MURMUR
MURMUR
LET'S GO DOWN, TOO.
...YEAH.

SNAP
!

MURMUR
MURMUR
...

DAMN IT! MIKU'S NOT HERE ANYMORE?
I GOT THROUGH TO ITSUKI! SHE SAYS SHE'S ON A BUS WITH MIKU!

Kyoto-Osaka Bus
京阪バス
稲荷大社前
Inari Taisha Stop
OH, THEN LET'S TAKE ONE, TOO.

...

UESUGI-SAN...
YOU HEARD WHAT I SAID...
...AT HE TOP F THE MOUN- TAIN, IDN'T YOU?

I DIDN'T HEAR ANYTHING.
AH!
YOU DEFI-NITELY HEARD!

I SAID I DIDN'T HEAR IT.
CAN'T WE JUST GO WITH THAT?

BUT...
...IT'S STILL TRUE THAT ME RUNNING MY MOUTH HURT MIKU.

SHE WORKED SO HARD...FOR SO LONG, FOR JUST THIS MOMENT...
AND...I'M THE ONE WHO GAVE ICHIKA THE IDEA TO DO THIS, TOO... DURING OUR FAMILY TRIP...

...
YEAH, IT'S YOUR FAULT.

CHECK AROUND YOU BEFORE SAYING... SOMETHING LIKE THAT.
SEE! I KNEW YOU HEARD...

WELL, I KNEW ALREADY.
HUH?
YOU KNEW?
...
HUH? WHAT DID YOU KNOW?
YOU KNOW...
HOW, UH...
...M-MIKU...
...HAS ...
...FEELINGS FOR ME.

I DON'T THINK I HEARD YOU RIGHT.
CAN YOU SAY THAT AGAIN?
STOP!
I'M NOT SAYING IT AGAIN!

THE OBLIVIOUS UESUGI-SAN KNEW... I DON'T BELIEVE IT...
...

WELL, A LOT HAPPENED.

SO I WAS PRETTY CON-FUSED WHEN SHE SAID SHE'D SUPPORT ME.

THE MIKU I TALKED TO THAT DAY WASN'T THE REAL HER.
I GUESS I WAS RIGHT ABOUT THAT.

?

SO DON'T WORRY ABOUT IT.
YOU WORRY TOO MUCH ABOUT OTHERS.

TO BE PERFECTLY FRANK, YOU TAKE IT TOO FAR.
AH... HAHA...
THAT'S FINE.
I TOLD YOU BEFORE HOW WHEN I FAILED, EVERYONE CAME WITH ME, RIGHT?
I DRAGGED EVERYONE INTO MY PROBLEMS.
THAT'S NOT SOMETHING I CAN MAKE UP FOR EASY.

SO IT'S ONLY NATURAL MY SISTERS END UP HAPPIER THAN ME.
YOU THINK SO?
I WANTED EVERYONE TO HAVE FUN ON THIS TRIP, TOO...
UESUGI-SAN...
IS THERE ANY WAY EVERYONE CAN END UP HAPPY?

IF EACH PERSON COULD FEEL HAPPY WITHOUT COMPARING THEMSELVES TO OTHERS...

IF WE COULD DO THAT, WE'D HAVE THE WORLD YOU'RE WISHING FOR.

Y-YES, YOU'RE RIGHT!
THEN-
BUT.

THINKING REALISTICALLY... IT'S NOT RARE AT ALL FOR SOME-ONE'S HAPPINESS TO MAKE SOMEONE ELSE UNHAPPY.

PEOPLE FIGHT AND TAKE THINGS FROM ONE ANOTHER.

SOME HAPPINESS IS WON THAT WAY.

WHEN YOU PUT IT THAT WAY, THEN I CAN DO...
NOTHING.

THERE'S A LIMIT.

DON'T YOU THINK IT'S A LITTLE PRE-SUMPTUOUS?
TRYING TO GET EVERY-THING.

WHEN YOU CHOOSE ONE THING...
...YOU DON'T CHOOSE ANOTHER.

THE DAY WILL COME WHEN A CHOICE HAS TO BE MADE.
SOME DAY.

わい
CHATTER
わい
CHATTER
わい
CHATTER

LISTEN TO ME, GIRLS.

I'M BEING PURSUED...
...BY A VOYEUR PHOTOGRAPHER.

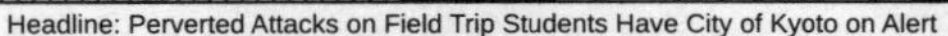
Headline: Perverted Attacks on Field Trip Students Have City of Kyoto on Alert

MUNCH
MUNCH
HUH?!

修学旅行生ねらった痴漢被害
京都市が注意喚起
I'VE SENSED THEM SINCE WE WERE AT KYOTO STATION.
I'M SURE ABOUT IT.
I EVEN SAW A NEWS STORY THE OTHER DAY ABOUT HOW STUDENTS ON FIELD TRIPS ARE BEING TARGETED.

EVEN IF THERE WAS ONE, WHY WOULD THEY TARGET YOU, NINO?
WH-WHAT'S THAT SUP-POSED TO MEAN?!
SNAP

!!
I KNEW IT!

WHAT A FEAST!
LET'S POST IT ON INSTA-GRAM!

I'M MORE CONCERNED WITH MIKU AND ICHIKA...
WE COULDN'T CATCH THEM BEFORE WE HAD TO COME BACK...
THEY DID AT LEAST COME BACK TO THE HOTEL, RIGHT?

YES, THEY BOTH APPEAR TO BE EXHAUSTED, SO THEY ARE RESTING IN OUR ROOM.
I HIGHLY DOUBT THEY'RE IN THE SAME ROOM.

I WONDER WHAT MADE MIKU SUDDENLY DECIDE TO GO OFF ON HER OWN...
THUNK

I THINK I'M GONNA GO CHECK ON HER AFTER ALL!

WAIT A MINUTE.

I'M ALMOST FINISHED EATING.
I'LL GO WITH YOU.
NINO...
I'm already finished!

I APOLOGIZE AGAIN, BUT I CANNOT STAND TOMATOES. WOULD YOU EAT THEM FOR ME AS WELL?
OH?
WHAT'S THE MATTER, UESUGI-KUN?

WHERE
HE...
MAEDA?
HE'S BEEN IN THE BATHROOM FOR QUITE A WHILE, HASN'T HE?
I THINK I'LL GO, TOO.
THEN I SUPPOSE I'LL BE GOING AS WELL.
DON'T FOLLOW ME.

KNOCK KNOCK

MIKU, ICHIKA, YOU'RE IN THERE, AREN'T YOU?
OPEN THE DOOR.
...

NO RE-SPONSE...
THEY'RE IGNORING THEIR PHONES, TOO...
THIS IS OUR ROOM TOO, YOU KNOW...

MIKU! I'M SORRY!
THIS IS ALL MY FAULT!

BUT THERE'S STILL TWO DAYS LEFT ON THE FIELD TRIP!
I WANT YOU TO LET ME MAKE IT UP TO YOU!

...
YOTSUBA DIDN'T DO ANYTHING WRONG...

YOTSU-BA...

FWIP

SNAP
!

HA... HA-HA...
YOU PUT THE THOUGHT IN MY HEAD, SO NOW I'M HEARING THINGS AS WELL, NINO...
Y-YEAH, THAT'S IT. WE'RE JUST HEARING THINGS, RIGHT?

THEY WOULDN'T POSSIBLY TRY IT INSIDE THE-

RMB
RMB
RMB
RMB
RMB
RMB
RMB
RMB
SNAP
STANDARD TYPE
EEEEEEEEEK!
SHIVER
SHIVER
SHIVER
SHIVER
SHIVER

WHUMP
WHAT WAS THAT SCREAM?!
WHAT HAP-PENED?!

!
...OH.

PHEW...
WE SHOULD BE SAFE HERE...
WHAT IN THE WORLD WAS THAT?
TUMP
TUMP
BRRRNG
CLICK
NINO, WAS THAT SCREAM-
FINALLY ANSWERED YOUR PHONE, EH?

ICHIKA, YOU...
FUTARO-KUN... I'M GLAD I RAN INTO YOU.
DO YOU HAVE SOME TIME TOMOR-ROW?
MIKU...
WHAT ARE YOU PLANNING TO DO TOMOR-ROW?

I NEED TO TELL YOU SOMETHING.

UGH... PLEASE DON'T TAKE MY PICTURE...
GLOW
CHAPTER 83
SISTERS' WAR: ROUND 5

OHHH, I CAN SEE ALL THE WAY TO THE STATION!
UGH... WHAT IF WE FALL?
I THOUGHT THE FENCE WAS HIGHER.
AH HA HA, WE'VE GOTTEN TALLER!
SHWIP
!!
GOTCHA.
HON-ESTLY! PLEASE DON'T DO THAT!
SORRY!
OU TWO ARE WFULLY NOISY.

WHOA.
IT FEELS PRETTY HIGH AFTER NOT SEEING IT FOR SO LONG.

HMM? UESUGI-KUN?
WE ARE SUPPOSED TO OPERATE IN GROUPS ON THE SECOND DAY...
YOUR FRIENDS AREN'T WITH YOU?

NO, I'VE GOT SOME BUSI-NESS WITH MIKU.

!
I FIGURED SHE'D BE WITH YOU.

MIKU IS NOT HERE.

ICHIKA AND NINO ARE APPARENTLY SEEING THE SIGHTS WITH THEIR FRIENDS FROM LAST YEAR.

MIKU IS RESTING IN THE HOTEL BECAUSE SHE STILL DOESN'T FEEL WELL.

WE'RE WORRIED ABOUT MIKU, BUT BECAUSE OF ALL THAT, THE TWO OF US ARE SEEING THE SIGHTS ALONE.
IT'S PRETTY SAD WHEN LESS THAN 50% OF YOU ARE HERE, HUH?

...

CLENCH
WH-WHAT'S THE PROBLEM EVERY ONCE IN A WHILE?
COME ON!
WE ARE AT KIYOMIZU-DERA AFTER ALL!

ITSUKI?
JUST LOOK AT THE VIEW, UESUGI-KUN. IT'S BREATH-TAKING.

D-DON'T PUSH ME.
THAT'S DANGER-OUS.

HEH HEH! ARE YOU AFRAID OF HEIGHTS?
A BOY LIKE YOU?

HUH? I-I'M NOT THE LEAST BIT SCARED!
YOU SURE YOU'RE OT THE ONE THAT'S CARED?
WH-WHAT ARE YOU TALKING ABOUT?!
OH! I LMOST ORGOT!

LET'S TAKE A PHOTO TOGETHER!
RIGHT HERE!
HUH?!
WHY?!
WILL YOU TAKE ONE OF US, YOTSUBA?
UH, SURE, I GUESS...
...
IF WE'RE DOING THIS, MAKE IT FAST.
O-OF COURSE!
SORRY FOR THE TROUBLE!

SQUEEZE

WHOA...
I CAN'T BELIEVE I'M BEING SO BOLD!

BUT! AFTER ALL THIS, SURELY UESUGI-KUN WILL REMEMBER WHAT HAPPENED SIX YEARS AGO!
...
COME TO THINK OF IT, WASN'T THAT PHOTO TAKEN HERE, TOO?
THEN SHE BOUGHT FIVE CHARMS AT THAT STAND...
OH, BUT DIDN'T THAT ONE GET SWEPT AWAY IN THE RIVER?
OH YEAH!!
WHAT'S THE MATTER?
DID YOU REMEMBER SOMETHING?

I'M SORRY FOR THE TROUBLE.
DON'T WORRY ABOUT IT. I JUST HATE THAT THIS HAD TO HAPPEN DURING YOUR FIELD TRIP.

I'LL REST A LITTLE MORE IN MY ROOM.

YES, AND IF YOU FEEL BETTER, LET ME KNOW.
OH, BEFORE I FORGET...

THERE SEEMS TO BE SOME WEIRDO TAKING ILLICIT PHOTOS IN THE HOTEL, SO BE CAREFUL.
...
THANK YOU, MA'AM.
THUNK

MYSTERI-OUS AS A SHADE...
...WAS IT?

WHAT ARE YOU DOING...
NINO?

ACTING LIKE YOU.
IN MORE WAYS THAN ONE.
THEY'D FOR SURE GET SUSPICIOUS IF TWO OF US PLAYED SICK.

THE NEXT ROLL CALL IS... YEP, I'VE GOT PLENTY OF TIME STILL.
I WAS ASKING WHY YOU CAME HERE...

DIDN'T I SAY ON THE PHONE?
I WANT TO TALK TO YOU ALONE.
...

IF YOU CAME TO CHEER ME UP, JUST FORGET IT.
WHY THE HELL WOULD I TRY TO CHEER YOU UP?
HUH?

MY RIVAL IN LOVE JUST BACKED DOW OF HER OWN ACCORD.
I CONSIDER THIS A LUCKY BREAK.
NOW I JUST HAVE TO BEAT ICHIKA.
HOW AM I GOING TO DEAL WITH THAT SNEAK...?
ANY-WAYS...
...I'M TAKING FU-KUN.
YOU OKAY WITH THAT?
FU-KUN...
WHEN DID YOU START-
WHAT? YOU'RE NOT GONNA TELL ME TO LET YOU HAVE HIM BECAUSE YOU LIKED HIM FIRST, ARE YOU?
TH-THAT'S NOT WHAT I WAS GETTING AT...

SURE, YOU MAY HAVE BEEN FIRST.
I'M STILL NOT SURE WHETHER TIME HAS ANY BEARING ON LOVE.
THIS IS THE FIRST TIME ANYTHING LIKE THIS HAS HAPPENED TO ME.
I'VE GOT ABSOLUTELY NO IDEA WHAT'S RIGHT OR WRONG.
ALL I'M SURE ABOUT IS THAT I LOVE HIM MORE THAN ANYONE ELSE.

I HAVEN'T... GIVEN UP EITHER.
WHEN YOU DECIDED TO WASTE YOUR CHANCE TO GET CLOSE TO HIM ON THIS FIELD TRIP...
...YOU BASICALLY GAVE UP.
YOUR TURN IS OVER. NICE GOING.
I DON'T WANT TO GIVE UP!
I KNEW THIS WAS GOING TO HAPPEN...
BUT WHEN FUTARO LEARNED HOW I FEEL, I STARTED THINKING HOW I'M NOT GOOD ENOUGH...
BUT I'M SCARED.
HE COULDN'T POSSIBLY LIKE SOME-ONE LIKE ME.

I HAD NO IDEA FIGHTING FAIR WOULD BE SO SCARY.

WHY ARE YOU STARTING WITH THE ASSUMPTION THAT YOU'LL LOSE?
THINKING LIKE THAT WILL MAKE IT HAPPEN FOR SURE!

WELL, I'M UP AGAINST ICHIKA...

SHE'S CUTE, SOCIABLE, POPULAR WITH THE BOYS...
SHE'S EVEN STRONG ENOUGH TO HAVE A DREAM FOR HER FUTURE.
IF I WERE A BOY, I'D CHOOSE ICHIKA.

PLUS...
THAT GOES FOR YOU, TOO, NINO...
!

YEAH, THANKS...

BUT I ALREADY KNEW I WAS CUTE!

WHICH GOES TO SHOW HOW WEIRD HE IS FOR NOT INSTANTLY SAYING YES WHEN I ASKED HIM OUT.
DOESN'T HE KNOW HOW MUCH COURAGE THAT TOOK?

WAIT, I GUESS I AM THE ONE WHO TOLD HIM TO POST-PONE HIS REPLY...
BUT HE STILL TICKS ME OFF!
YOU EVEN ASKED HIM OUT...

YOU'RE AMAZING, NINO.
I GUESS THAT MEANS YOU HAVEN'T YET?
THAT DOPE WON'T GET IT UNLESS YOU TELL HIM.

WELL...
I DID... TECHNICAL-LY...
EVEN THOUGH HE DIDN'T REALIZE I MEANT IT...

BUT AT THIS POINT...
...I DON'T EVEN HAVE THE CON-FIDENCE TO DO IT AGAIN.

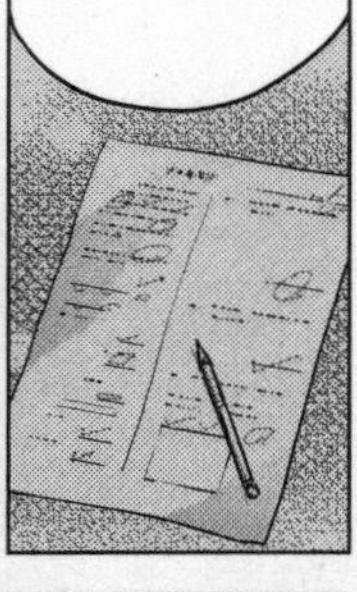
I'LL DO IT IF I GET THE TOP SCORE ON THE TEST...

I'LL DO IT IF I BAKE TASTY BREAD...

I'M THE ONE WHO KEPT PUTTING IT OFF LIKE THAT.
IT'S NOT ICHIKA'S FAULT... OR ANYONE ELSE'S...
I BROUGHT IT ON MYSELF.

OH YEAH?
THEN JUST KEEP MOPING FOREVER.

YOU JUST KEEP DRAGGING YOUR FEET...
I DON'T GET YOU AT ALL.

BUT I STILL...

...THOUGHT OF YOU...
...AS MY RIVAL.
!
WE WOULDN'T EVEN BE A FAIR MATCH?
HUH? I JUST CALLED YOU MY RIVAL IN LOVE.

YOU ADMITTED I WAS CUTE RIGHT AWAY.
SO WHAT'S YOUR PROBLEM ?!
THINK ABOUT IT.
WE'RE QUINTU-PLETS.

THAT MEANS YOU'RE CUTE, TOO!

WAIT A SECOND! DON'T YOU THINK THIS'S TOO SHORT?!
YOU'RE THE ONE WHO TOLD ME TO CUT IT.
I DID, BUT... I'VE NEVER HAD IT CUT THIS SHORT BEFORE...
IT'S OKAY. IT'S CUTE.
I-IT BET-TER BE!
YEP, YOU LOOK CUTE.

SEE YA!
THUNK
NINO...
I'M SORRY...

Above: Matchmaking Charms, Below: Prayers for Luck

UM... DO YOU HAPPEN TO KNOW WHERE UESUGI-KUN WENT?
良縁祈願
HE JUST KIND OF VANISHED ON US, HUH?
I'M SURE HE WENT BACK TO HIS FRIENDS.

ITSUKI~ THEY'VE GOT LOVE CHARMS! AREN'T THEY CUTE?
LET'S BUY ONE FOR MIKU!

THIS WAS A PERFECT CHANCE...
WHAT SHOULD I DO?

ARE YOU...
...HIDING SOMETHING FROM ME?
...!

TMP たっ
TMP たっ
TMP たっ

H-
HEY!
WHERE ARE YOU TAKING ME?

DON'T WORRY ABOUT IT.
JUST COME ALONG.

WHAT'S GOTTEN INTO YOU?
...

MIKU...

LISTEN TO WHAT MIKU HAS TO SAY.
IF FUTARO-KUN KNOWS MIKU LIKES HIM, IT CONTRADICTS MY LIE.

I'LL USE ANYTHING I CAN.

THIS IS ALL I HAVE LEFT.

THIS IS THE ONLY WAY I CAN WIN THIS BATTLE!
RMB
RMB

CHAPTER 83
SISTERS' WAR: ROUND 6

YOU'VE...
...BEEN HERE BEFORE, HAVEN'T YOU?

YEAH...
WHEN I WAS IN ELEMEN-TARY SCHOOL.

WHEN YOU WERE IN ELEMENTARY SCHOOL?

I REMEM-BER IT LIKE IT WAS YESTERDAY.

THAT GIRL... RENA, SHE DRAGGED ME AROUND ALL OVER THE PLACE.

HOW COULD MY TRIP WITH HER, WHO SAID SHE NEEDED ME, NOT BE FUN?

BEFORE WE KNEW IT, THE SUN HAD SET...AND IT WAS DARK OUT.

THEN WHAT HAP-PENED?

ONE OF THE TEACHERS WAS SENT TO PICK ME UP.

THEY LET ME WAIT IN AN EMPTY ROOM AT THE INN WHERE RENA WAS STAYING.
I THINK WE PLAYED CARDS.
MY HOME-ROOM TEACHER REALLY TORE ME A NEW ONE.

BUT NOW, I CONSIDER THOSE GOOD MEMORIES.

THAT GIRL WAS-
DON'T YOU THINK THAT'S ENOUGH?
HUH?

I THOUGHT YOU MIGHT HAVE SOMETHING IN MIND, SO I TOLD YOU THE STORY...
...BUT NOW I'M OVER IT.

I'M THROUGH GOING ALONG WITH THIS FARCE...
MIKU. NO...
ICHIKA.
HUH?! WHAT THE?! HOW DID YOU-
A HUNCH.
HUUUH?!
JUST BASED ON THE SITUATION WE'RE IN...
...I FIG-URED THE CHANCES WERE HIGHEST IT WAS YOU.
HUH?
Y- YOU'RE WRONG!
SORRY!
AND...
I'VE GOT NO REASON TO STICK AROUND FOR YOUR LITTLE SKITS.

SEE? I'M RIGHT.
RUSTLE
...!
PLIP
PLIP
RMB
RMB
THIS TIMING...
I IMAGINE IT'S SAFE TO SAY YOU'RE THE "MIKU" I SPOKE TO IN THE HALL AT SCHOOL THE OTHER DAY, TOO?
HH
HH
SHH
TH-THAT WASN'T-
WHY DID YOU LIE TO ME LIKE THAT?
PLAP
PLAP
PLAP

ZSHHHHHHH
WHAT WE WERE TALKING ABOUT...
DON'T YOU KNOW, FUTARO-KUN...
...THAT THE GIRL YOU MET SIX YEARS AGO WAS ONE OF US?
...YEAH.
...IT WAS ME.
SHE...
SHE WAS ME...
WE MET SIX YEARS AGO...

IT'S TRUE...
BELIEVE ME...
...
HEY, YOU TWO!
THE SIGHT SEEING'S BEEN CALLED OFF! WE'RE GOING BACK TO THE HOTEL!
DO YOU REMEMBER THE CHARMS WE BOUGHT HERE TOGETHER THAT DAY?
HUH?! OF COURSE!
I STILL HAVE IT!
HOW COULD I FORGET?
SO...
YOU'RE LYING TO ME.
ZSHHHHHHHH
SORRY. I CAN'T BELIEVE A WORD YOU SAY RIGHT NOW.
LET'S GO BACK BEFORE WE CATCH COLDS.

FOR NOW, WE WANT YOU TO CHANGE INTO DRY CLOTHES AND WAIT IN YOUR ROOMS WITH YOUR GROUPS.
AW~ ...
WE CAME ALL THE WAY TO KYOTO TO SIT IN THE HOTEL?

DIDN'T THE FORECAST SAY IT WAS GONNA BE SUNNY?
WE GOT SOME KINDA RAIN MAGNET WITH US, HUH? WELL, THEY BETTER NOT SHOW THEIR FACE AROUND ME! YOU HEAR THAT?!
WHERE WERE YOU, UESUGI-KUN?

OH... I HAD A LITTLE BUSINESS TO TAKE CARE OF.
HAHAHA! YOU MUST'VE GOTTEN LOST.

WHAT ARE WE GONNA DO TOMORROW?
...

シャー
SHHHHH
キュッ
SKREEK
I'M OUT OF THE SHOWER.
SORRY TO GO FIRST.

TH- THEN ...
YOU CAN GO NEXT, YOTSUBA ...
UGH...
I'M SOAKED DOWN TO MY UNDIES...
LOOKS LIKE I WAS RIGHT NOT TO GO.
...

WOW! THOSE ARE PRETTY GUTSY, ITSUKI-CHAN. YOU AREN'T GOING TO WEAR THEM?
N-NO! THESE AREN'T FOR WEARING!
THEY DON'T FIT ME, SO I PLAN TO THROW THEM OUT!
ICHIKA.
DON'T YOU HAVE SOMETHING TO SAY TO MIKU?

OH...
SORRY...
ICHIKA.
KNOCK
KNOCK
COM-
ING
IN.
!

CHAC
IS EVERYONE IN GROUP FIVE HERE?
WE'RE APPARENTLY MEETING IN THE BIG HALL ON THE SECOND FLOOR IN THIRTY MINUTES FOR INFORMATION.

WHAT ARE YOU DOING...?
WELL, I AM THE CLASS OFFICER...

ARE YOU-
TMP
TMP
B-BATH-ROOM!
TMP

THUNK

...

ARE YOU GIRLS STILL FIGHTING?
TELL ME ABOUT IT.
HUH?! UM...
THIS IS-

PHEW! MUCH BETTER!
STEAM
STEAM
THUNK
WHAM!
...
GASP!

I-IT'S NO BIG DEAL, RIGHT?
RIGHT!
SISTERS FIGHT LIKE THIS ALL THE TIME.
TH-TH-THAT'S JUST COMMON SENSE.

I HOPE SO...

ANYWAY, BE THERE IN THIRTY MINUTES.
APPARENTLY, WE'LL BE DECIDING WHICH COURSE WE WANT TO TAKE THERE, SO GIVE IT SOME THOUGHT.
!

THUNK
...

SORRY...
...FOR HANDLING IT MY WAY...
IT'S FINE. HAVING FU-KUN WORRY ABOUT US IS THE THING I WANT TO AVOID MOST.

AND DON'T JUST RUN AWAY LIKE THAT, MIKU.
WELL...
MIKU...YOU CANNOT ACT LIKE THIS FOREVER.

...
LET'S CLEAR THE AIR, GIRLS.

WE'RE ALL LOOKING FOR OPPORTUNITIES TO GET ALONE WITH FUTARO-KUN.

I TOLD YOU THAT BACK WHEN WE SELECTED GROUPS.
DOES THAT GO FOR YOU TOO, ITSUKI?

...
I CANNOT DENY IT...

AT THIS RATE, NO ONE'S GONNA MAKE ANY HEADWAY.
AND I KNOW NONE OF US WANT THAT.

YOU'RE THE ONE TELLING US THIS?
YOU LISTEN TOO, YOTSUBA.
HE'S GONE, RIGHT?
THE FINAL DAY...
YOUR CHOICE OF ONSITE LEARNING COURSES.
3日目選択別コース
Bコース 名庭巡り
Cコース 茶道体験
Dコース 織田信長のゆかりの地巡り
Eコース 太秦映画村
* Day Three Course Selection
YOU KNOW WE'RE GIVEN THE CHOICE OF FIVE DIFFERENT PLACES WE CAN GO TO LEARN, RIGHT?
WHY DON'T WE EACH CHOOSE ONE OF THE FIVE?
A
B
C
D
E
WE'LL LEAVE WHO GETS THEIR CHANCE WITH FUTARO-KUN UP TO THE ONE WHO LUCKS OUT AND PICKS THE SAME COURSE AS HIM.
LET'S LEAVE THE FINAL DECISION...
...TO FATE.

SECOND!
THIS WAY THERE'LL BE NO HARD FEELINGS!
FWAP
I DON'T LIKE IT!
WHY ARE YOU PROPOSING THIS PLAN AFTER ALL THE SNEAK-ING AROUND YOU'VE DONE?

ARE YOU OKAY WITH THIS?
IT'S ONLY A ONE IN FIVE CHANCE.

I DON'T EVEN KNOW...HOW I'M SUPPOSED TO FACE HIM RIGHT NOW.
SO I PREFER HAVING A LOW CHANCE...

I THINK... THIS IS THE BEST OPTION.
WE SHOULD HAVE DONE IT FROM THE BEGINNING.

RIGHT...
WE CAN JUST POINT, RIGHT?
WE'LL PROBABLY ALL PICK DIFFERENT THINGS LIKE ALWAYS.

ON THREE...

Name
Ichika Nakano (E) Course
HEY, UESUGI, WHAT DO YOU WAN-NA PICK TOMOR-ROW?
LET'S GO WITH E.
THIS ISN'T WHAT I MEANT WHEN I SAID IT.
I WANTED TO BE HAPPY FOR YOU!
SORRY...
ICHIKA.

IT'S THE FINAL DAY ALREADY?
I'M GLAD IT'S SUNNY.
LET'S HAVE ENOUGH FUN TO MAKE UP FOR YESTER-DAY!

STUDENTS TAKING THE A COURSE GATHER 'ROUND!
GLANCE
キョロ
GLANCE
キョロ
A

I KNEW...
...I SHOULDN'T HAVE LEFT IT UP TO CHANCE.

THOSE GO-ING ON THE B COURSE LINE UP OVER HERE.
YOU AREN'T HERE, ARE YOU, UESUGI-SAN?

C
...

D

I JUST KIND OF PICKED ONE AT RANDOM... WHERE DO WE GO FOR COURSE D?
YOU KNOW, IT'S THE HISTORY ONE. WE GO SEE THINGS LIKE HONNOJI TEMPLE AND THE GRAVES OF WAR-LORDS AND STUFF.

WHAT?! I DON'T CARE ABOUT ANY OF THAT...

YOU SHOULD HAVE CHECKED BEFORE-
OH.
YOU LIKE JAPANESE HISTORY TOO, HUH?

ICHIKA-SAN...
...
MY STOMACH HURTS...
COURSE E IS THIS WAY.
WE'RE ABOUT TO LEAVE.
E

OH.

CHAPTER 84
SISTERS' WAR: ROUND 7
STUDENTS WHO CHOSE THE E COURSE FOR THE FINAL DAY OF THE FIELD TRIP...
...WE HAVE JUST REACHED OUR DESTINATION FOR TODAY...
...KYOTO STUDIO PARK.
ICHIKA SHOULD HAVE BEEN HERE...
I'D RATHER TAKE THE D COURSE.
TRADE WITH ME, MIKU.
THAT WAS PRETTY INTERESTING, WASN'T IT?
WHY DID SHE ASK TO TRADE WITH ME?
I HEARD WE'LL GET TO LOOK AROUND UNTIL THIS AFTERNOON.
WHERE THE HELL ARE WE GOIN'? HUH?!
!

...

OH, NAKANO-SAN! WE MEET AGAIN.
!

STMP
STMP
HAHA! SHE RAN AWAY AGAIN.
I THINK SHE HATES YOU, DUDE.

!

MIKU! WAIT A-
BUMP
OH!

HEY, ARE YOU OKAY?
SORRY ABOUT THAT.

YOU'VE GOTTA WATCH WHERE YOU'RE GOING.

POOF

WHUMP
I'M SORRY, NINO!

I CAN'T DO IT...
THIS IS SO AWK-WARD...

S-SEE YOU.
SHK

OH! WAIT!

WOULD YOU LIKE TO TRY ON THE CLOTHING OF A SENGOKU PERIOD WAR-LORD?
FREEZE

...

Sign: (top) Historical Dramas, (bottom) House of Disguise

WHAT'S ALL THIS ABOUT?
NOT ONLY DIDN'T THEY HAVE WARLORD COSTUMES.
...BUT TAKEDA AND MAEDA ARE TAKING FOREVER TO PUT THEIRS ON.
AND MIKU SAID SHE'D WAIT HERE, BUT SHE'S VANISHED...
SHE MUST'VE RUN OFF AGAIN...
I GUESS THAT'S ONLY NATURAL AFTER WHAT HAPPENED ON THE FIRST DAY...

OH.
SO YOU TRIED A COSTUME, TOO?
I WASN'T PLANNING TO...
...BUT THE LADY IN CHARGE WAS SUPER EXCITED ABOUT IT...
...AND BEFORE I KNEW WHAT HIT ME...
I prepared this for you.

DO I...
...LOOK WEIRD?
...
O, YOU LOOK FINE.

!
WH-WHERE ARE YOUR FRIENDS?
TH- THEY'RE STILL IN THERE.
YEESH, THOSE TWO ARE HOPELESS.

HUH? I SAW THEM WALKING OUT BEFORE I CHANGED.
HUH?
SO THEY WERE SO EXCITED THEY COULDN'T WAIT?
WHY DON'T YOU CALL THEM?
YEAH, I'LL DO THAT.

I DON'T KNOW THEIR NUMBERS...
ARE YOU REALLY FRIENDS?

I DOUBT THEY MADE IT VERY FAR...
AND, AT THE VERY WORST, I'LL JUST HAVE TO CHECK THE LOST CHILDREN CENTER.

MIKU...
WOULD YOU HELP ME LOOK FOR THEM?

I DEFINITELY DON'T HAVE THE COURAGE TO WALK AROUND IN THIS GETUP ALONE.
BUT YOU DON'T WANT TO BE ALONE WITH ME THE WHOLE TIME, DO YOU?

LET'S FIND THEM QUICK THEN HAVE SOME FUN.
IT'S GOING TO SUCK IF OUR ONLY MEMORIES OF THE THIRD DAY ARE OF LOOKING FOR PEOPLE.
O-OKAY.

日本橋
江戸屋

SPLASH
FUTARO, GET A PICTURE!
BEFORE IT GOES BACK UNDER!
ALL RIGHT, FINE.

NOW MY COSTUME'S SOAKED!

YOU WARNED ME, BUT YOU'RE THE ONE WHO NEEDS TO PAY MORE ATTENTION TO WHAT'S GOING ON AROUND YOU, FUTARO!

I ALREADY APOLOGIZED, DIDN'T I? MORE THAN ONCE.

THAT'S WEIRD... IT FELT LIKE SOMEONE PUSHED ME...

I'LL GO APOLOGIZE TO THE LADY IN CHARGE...
...SO YOU GO AHEAD AND CHANGE.
OKAY.
WAIT...
I STARTED TALKING TO HIM LIKE NORMAL BEFORE I REALIZED IT...
SO MUCH HAPPENED, BUT... SOMEHOW...
WHEN I'M WITH FUTARO, IT FEELS LIKE I'M GOING TO FORGET ABOUT ALL THE SMALL STUFF.
YES...
THINGS LIKE...

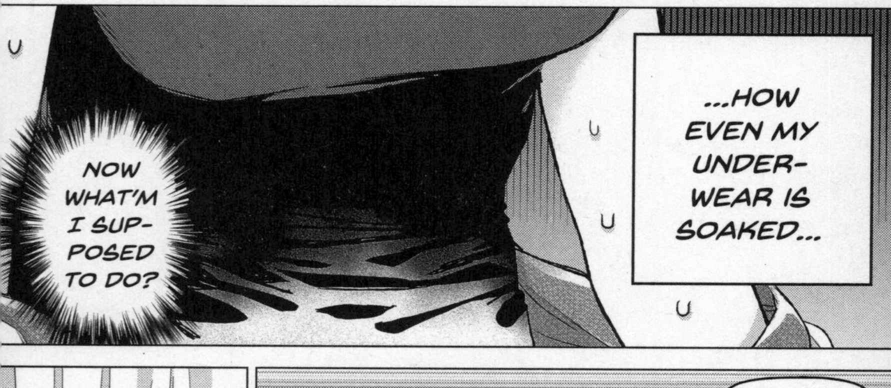
...HOW EVEN MY UNDER-WEAR IS SOAKED...
NOW WHAT'M I SUP-POSED TO DO?

NO, REALLY, WHAT DO I DO? I CAN'T WEAR THESE...
AT THIS RATE...
SHOULD I CALL THAT LADY IN CHARGE?
OH, I DO HAVE MY TIGHTS... MAYBE I CAN JUST-
WAIT, WHAT AM I THINKING?! NO WAY, NO HOW!
す
FWIP
!

Please use these if you need them.
HUH? THIS IS...
...A BAG FROM AN UNDER-WEAR STORE?
WHO IN THE...?
WAS IT THAT LADY IN CHARGE?
THEN I'LL GLADLY WEAR-

OH...

I STILL HAVEN'T SEEN THOSE TWO AROUND...
MAN, WHERE'D THEY RUN OFF TO?

FLINCH
HMM? WHAT'S THE MATTER, MIKU?

WHOA!
THE WIND'S SO STRONG!
~~~~!
WHOOOOOSH

I'M TIRED...
LET'S SIT DOWN FOR A BIT...

~~~~

YEP.
THINGS WERE SO HECTIC THESE THREE DAYS HAVE JUST FLOWN BY, HUH?
ALTHOUGH IT WAS REALLY ONLY TWO DAYS FOR ME...
BUT I DON'T MIND.
I GOT TO SPEND THE END WITH YOU, FUTARO.
THAT'S ENOUGH FOR ME.
MIKU...

WHAT'S THAT?
?

HUH?!
WHAT'S MY BREAD DOING HERE?
HUH, SO YOU MADE THIS?
ドキ
ドキ
BA-DUMP
BA-DUMP
I DID... BUT...
...I THOUGHT I LOST THIS ON THE FIRST DAY OF THE TRIP...
WHAT'S IT DOING HERE?

I AM HUNGRY, SO I'LL TAKE ONE.
!
RUSTLE
OH!
FLOP...
THAT'S TOO OLD TO-
ZOOM
CHOMP
MUNCH
MUNCH
GULP

THAT WAS GOOD.

BUT PEOPLE TELL ME MY TONGUE'S DEFECTIVE.
SO I'M NOT ESPECIALLY CONFIDENT IN THAT JUDG-MENT.
THAT BREAD MIGHT HAVE TASTED BAD.
SO I CAN'T GIVE YOU ANY REAL FEEDBACK...

...BUT I CAN TASTE...
...THE EFFORT YOU PUT INTO IT.
YOU WORKED HARD, DIDN'T YOU?
...YEAH!

I WORKED REALLY HARD.

MY MOM USED TO BAKE BREAD FOR US.

EVERY DAY. UNTIL SHE DIED WHEN I WAS ABOUT SIX...

FOR SOME REASON, I JUST REMEMBERED THAT.

!
YOUR MOTHER...

SOME POPULAR, HANDMADE BREAD LIKE THEY SERVE AT SMALL, INDIVIDUAL CAFÉS.

ME AND DAD BOTH LOVED IT...

WAIT. NOBODY WANTS TO LISTEN TO ME RAMBLING ABOUT MY-SELF, RIGHT?
NO!
I WANT TO HEAR MORE!

WE'VE BEEN STUDYING TOGETHER SO LONG, BUT I DIDN'T KNOW ANYTHING ABOUT THAT!
I WAS SO WORRIED ABOUT MYSELF THAT I DIDN'T EVEN TR TO FIND OUT.
I WANT TO KNOW MORE ABOUT YOU...
...EVERY-THING ABOUT YOU, FUTARO!
AND...
...I WANT YOU TO KNOW EVERYTHING ABOUT ME, TOO!

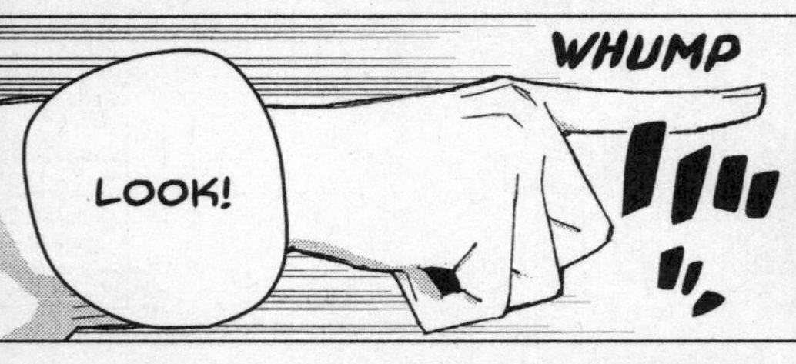

THAT'S A FAMOUS PLACE THAT GETS USED AS A MAGISTRATE'S OFFICE IN ALL SORTS OF HISTORICAL DRAMAS.

I'M HAPPY JUST GETTING TO SEE THAT TODAY.

THERE AREN'T AS MANY AS THE D COURSE, BUT THERE ARE PLENTY OF THINGS HERE I LOVE.

YEAH, THAT'S YOUR KIND OF THING.

I KNOW THAT.

I LOVE THAT BIG BRIDGE WE CROSSED JUST NOW, TOO.
THEY USE IT IN DRAMAS, TOO?
YEP, AND—

I LOVE THAT.
I LOVE THAT.
I LOVE THIS.

MAN, THAT SEEMS LIKE A LOT.
ALTHOUGH I DID KNOW THIS ALREADY.

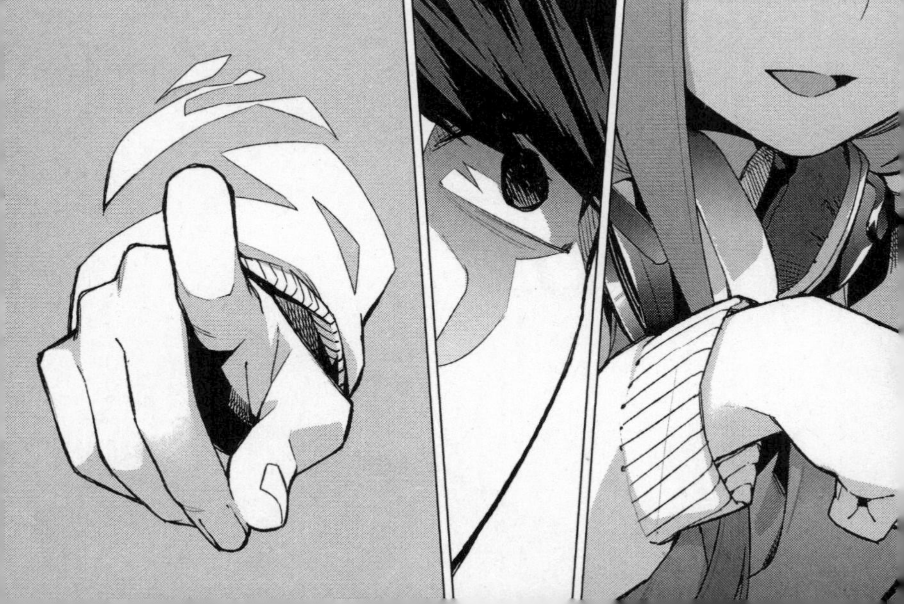

I LOVE YOU.

YEAH.
I KNOW.

CHAPTER 85
SISTERS' WAR: ROUND 7 (BEHIND THE SCENES)

I DON'T THINK THIS WILL EARN YOUR FORGIVE-NESS, BUT-
OH, SHE'S TRYING TO RUN AGAIN...
IS THERE ANYTHING AROUND...
...THAT WOULD GET HER ATTENTION?
OH, THAT'S IT!
WOULD YOU LIKE TO TRY ON THE CLOTHING OF A SENGOKU PERIOD WARLORD?
RUSTLE
!!
ICHIKA?! WHAT ARE YOU DOING HERE?!
I COULD ASK THE SAME OF YOU, NINO...
I FAKED BEING SICK SO I COULD AT LEAST MAKE SURE THINGS GO RIGHT FOR THOSE TWO...
DON'T TELL ME YOU'RE HERE TO GET IN MIKU'S WAY A-
N-NO!
I LEFT THE GROUP WITH STOMACH PAIN!

*Historical Dramas / House of Disguise

ALTHOUGH I'M SURE YOU WON'T BELIEVE ME...
EVEN IF WHAT I DID WAS UNFORGIV-ABLE...
...I WANT YOU TO LET ME MAKE UP FOR WHAT I'VE DONE AT LEAST A LITTLE ON THIS LAST DAY.

SINCE I'M SURE THIS IS PROBABLY GOING TO BE OUR LAST TRIP...
!

DON'T TELL ME YOU--
RUSTLE
RUSTLE

HUH?!
ICHIKA AND NINO ARE HERE, TOO!
SO WE ALL ENDED UP ON THE E COURSE?

YOU GIRLS, TOO?

YEESH... NO ONE FOLLOWED THE RULES.

OH.

IT LOOKS LIKE THEY'RE ON THEIR WAY.
W-WELL, WE'D BETTER FOLLOW THEM.
OKAY!
ALL RIGHT! LET'S ALL SUPPORT MIKU!

* Historical Dramas House of Disguise

DO YOU THINK THEY WILL...TRY ON COS-TUMES?
I KNOW FU-KUN WILL LOOK GOOD. I MEAN, HE'S GOT A HANDSOME FACE.
DIDN'T YOU SAY HE WASN'T YOUR TYPE OR SOME-THING AT FIRST?

HUH? WHAT ARE YOU TALKING ABOUT? I DON'T REMEMBER ANCIENT HISTORY.

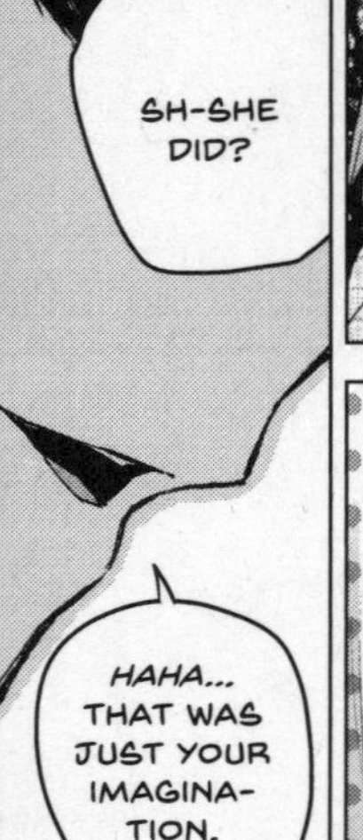

SH-SHE DID?
HAHA... THAT WAS JUST YOUR IMAGINA-TION.

ALTHOUGH I REMEMBER ICHIKA PAYING ATTENTION TO HIM FROM THE VERY START.

BECAUSE IT WAS THAT NIGHT THAT I REMEM-BERED...

...
WHAT'S THE MATTER, NINO?

THOSE TWO GUYS ARE IN THE WAY.
I'LL GO TAKE CARE OF THEM.
HUH?
TAKE CARE OF THEM?

AND SINCE THEY'RE HERE, YOU MAKE SURE MIKU TRIES A COSTUME, TOO.
SHK
H-
HOW AM I SUPPOSED TO DO THAT?

WELL, NATURAL-LY...
...SINCE YOU'VE GOT-TEN SO MUCH PRACTICE...
...YOU'LL DISGUISE YOURSELF AS HER.

...
YOU JERK...

EXCUSE ME.

I THINK I WOULD LIKE TO TRY ON A COSTUME AFTER ALL.

OF COURSE!
WHICH WOULD YOU LIKE TO WEAR?
OH, I'LL TAKE THIS CUTE ONE.
I'LL PREPARE IT RIGHT AWAY! WAIT HERE JUST A MOMENT!

GRAHHH!

WHOA!
IS UESUGI-KUN... REALLY IN HERE?

EEEEEK!
パン CLAP
パン CLAP
DISTRACTION SUCCESSFUL.

LOOKS LIKE ICHIKA PULLED IT OFF, TOO.
HUH... THEY LOOK GREAT TOGETHER.

WHOA!
FUTAR GET A PICTURE
BEFORE IT GOES BACK UNDER!
ALL RIGHT, FINE.
TMP
TMP
TMP
TMP

THIS DOESN'T MEAN I'M LETTING HER HAVE YOU...

HUH?! WHAT HAPPENED?

ARGH!

ARGH!

I'M NOT SURE, BUT I THINK SOMEONE FELL IN THE POND...

WAS THAT MIKU?

WHO JUST RAN UP TO THEM?

I THINK THAT WAS MIKU...
SHE'S AS SOAKED AS WE WERE YESTERDAY...
WHAT'S SHE GONNA DO ABOUT HER UNDERWEAR?
!
AT THIS RATE, MIKU'LL BE ON A COMMANDO DATE!
DO YOU THINK THEY SELL UNDERWEAR HERE?
M-MAYBE LOIN-CLOTHS?
Y-YOTSUBA, YOU GO CHECK WITH YOUR QUICK FEET!
BUT I DON'T THINK A LOINCLOTH IS--
IF THAT'S ALL WE CAN GET, WE'LL HAVE TO TAKE IT!
U-
UM...
I KNOW THIS SEEMS UM... STRANG ...
...BUT I THOUGHT IT WAS BEST TO BE PRE-PARED FOR ANYTHING, SO...
...I HAVE A SPARE PAIR OF UNDER-WEAR.
WHY?
OH...
STMP すた
すた STMP
すた STMP

KA-CLUNK
AS WE ARE UNDER MAIN-TENANCE, ONLY AUTHORIZED PERSONNEL ARE ALLOWED BEYOND THIS POINT.
MY SINCEREST APOLOGIES.
THAT SHOULD DO IT.
NINO.
SORRY I'M LATE.
HOW ARE THEY DOING NOW?

PROBA-BLY...
...PRETTY WELL.

YOTSU-BA...
WHAT SHOULD WE DO NOW?
OH!
I KNOW!

WAIT A SECOND...

I FOUND MIKU'S BREAD, BUT I LEFT IT AT THE HOTEL!
HUUUH?! BR-BREAD?!

IT'S ALL RIGHT.

I JUST NEED TO GIVE THIS TO MIKU, RIGHT?

RUSTLE

DIDN'T MIKU BAKE THAT BREAD?

YEAH... ON THE FIRST DAY OF THE TRIP, FOR UESUGI-SAN...
SHE HAD ME TASTE TESTING THE WHOLE TIME...

IF THAT HADN'T HAPPENED...
OH.

WAIT, I'M SORRY!
I'M NOT BLAMING YOU, ICHIKA...

...ANYWAY, I'M SORRY.
?

I... WANTED EVERYONE TO END UP HAPPY...

...SO I MAY HAVE BEEN CHEERING FOR THE ONE WHO'S USUALLY SO PASSIVE...

BUT I WOULD'VE REALIZED THIS WOULD HAPPEN IF I THOUGHT ABOUT IT A LITTLE...

I DIDN'T NOTICE YOUR TRUE FEELINGS, ICHIKA.

SO I'M SORRY.

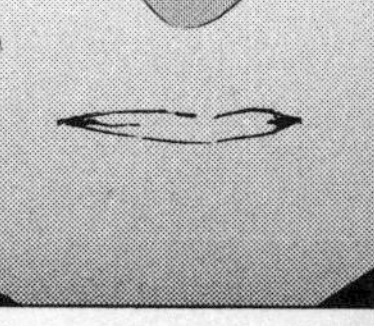

EVERYONE... KEEPS APOLOGIZING TO ME.

EVEN THOUGH I'M THE ONE WHO NEEDS TO APOLOGIZE THE MOST...

I WANT YOU TO KNOW EVERYTHING ABOUT ME, TOO!
!!
...
SORRY, MIKU.
I'M SORRY I KEPT GETTING IN YOUR WAY.
FUTARO-KUN...
I'M SORRY I KEPT LYING TO YOU.
BUT THAT-

LISTEN TO THIS, EVERY-BODY!
I MET A REALLY FUNNY BOY TODAY!
AND WE BOUGHT GOOD LUCK CHARMS TOGETHER!
I HEARD THEY TOOK HIM TO THE BIG HALL HERE!
...
OH.
YO!
CAME TO VISIT, HUH?
I WAS SO BORED BY MYSELF.
LET'S PLAY SOME-THING.
O-OH...
HOW ABOUT SEVENS?

I'M GONNA GOBBLE YOU UP!!
FUTARO.
YOTSUBA'S HERE, TOO.
ICHIKA AND MIKU!
OH, JUST TWO PEOPLE WHO ALREADY KNOW OUR TRICKS?
WHAT A WASTE OF A SCARE.
WHOA!
WHAT A SHOCK.
YOU SCARED ME.
THANKS FOR THAT.

W-
WE...
...MET SIX YEARS AGO...
I KNOW IT WAS ONLY...
...FOR A FEW SHORT MIN-UTES...
BUT I'M SURE THAT IT WAS BECAUSE WE SPENT THAT TIME TOGETHER...
...THAT I FELL FOR YOU.

I LOVE YOU.
...!
SHE TOLD HIM...
FUTARO-KUN MAY NOT BELIEVE A WORD I SAY ANYMORE...
...BUT THOSE...
THOSE MEMORIES ALONE ARE TRUE.

SAY, ICHIKA...
WHEN I SAW THE TWO OF THEM TOGETHER...
...I COULDN'T CONTROL MY-SELF. BEFORE I KNEW IT, I WAS RUNNING AT THEM.
I CRITICIZED YOU SO MUCH, BUT I TRIED TO GET IN MIKU'S WAY, TOO...
HOW PATHETIC...
NINO...
I UNDER-STAND HOW YOU FELT A LITTLE.
MAYBE IF THE TIMING HAD BEEN A LITTLE DIFFER-ENT...
...YOU WOULD'VE BEEN THE ONE YELL-ING AT ME.

SORRY I TALKED SO BIG.
NO...
THAT'S NOT TRUE.
THANKS.
BUT I REALIZED AT THE SAME TIME HOW STUPID I WAS.
DIDN'T YOU?
TILL THE VERY END...
...MIKU SAID YOU WEREN'T TO BLAME.
...YEAH.

GETTING HEAD STARTS...
HOLDING EACH OTHER BACK...

THERE'S NO MEANING TO ANY OF THIS FIGHTING.

WE AREN'T ENEMIES.

DON'T CALL THIS THE END...
LET'S APOLOGIZE TO MIKU.
I'M SURE WE'LL BE EVEN CLOSER THAN BEFORE.

THIS IS ONE OF THOSE RARE TIMES...
...WE CAN TALK ABOUT SOMETHING WE ALL LIKE.

CHAPTER 86
SISTERS' WAR: EXHIBITION MATCH
I LOVE YOU.
YEAH.
I KNOW.
BUT–
YEP.

I DEFINITELY LOVE ALL...
HUH?
...OF MY FAMILY.
HUUUUH?

HUUUH?!
OH.

WHAT ARE YOU GIRLS DOING HERE...?
YOU NOTICED, MIKU?
HOW LONG HAVE YOU KNOWN?

I KNEW IT...
I THOUGHT SOMETHING WAS UP WHEN I HEARD ICHIKA AND NINO'S VOICES.

WAIT, WAIT, WAIT...
LET'S SORT THIS OUT.

SO WHEN YOU...
...JUST SAID "I LOVE YOU"...

I WAS POINTING AT MY SISTERS, WHO WERE BEHIND YOU.
HMM?
DON'T TELL ME...
DID YOU THINK I WAS TALKING ABOUT YOU, MR. OVERSIZED EGO?

BLUUUSH

I-IT'S NOT NICE MAKING FUN OF PEOPLE!
ARE YOU SURE ABOUT THIS, MIKU? YOU FINALLY TOLD HIM HOW YOU FEEL, BUT NOW YOU'RE PLAYING IT OFF LIKE A JOKE...
IT'S ALL RIGHT.
I'M NOT STUPID ENOUGH TO CHARGE IN WHEN I'VE GOT NO CHANCE OF WINNING LIKE A CERTAIN SOMEONE.
WHO ARE YOU CALLING STUPID?
AND...

FUTARO'S NOT AS OBLIVIOUS AS YOU THINK.
...
I GUESS... THAT DOES MAKE SENSE...
SO, YO-TSUBA...
...THANKS FOR THE BREAD.
HEH HEH HEH!
FOR A MINUTE THERE, I DIDN'T THINK IT'D WORK OUT!
ITSUKI... THESE WERE PROBABLY FROM YOU, RIGHT?
THANKS...
I'M SORRY...
NINO.
FORGET IT. WE'RE SISTERS.

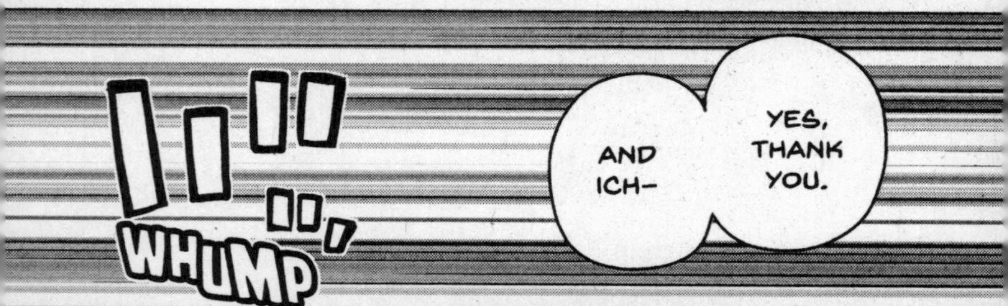

YES, THANK YOU.
AND ICH-
WHUMP

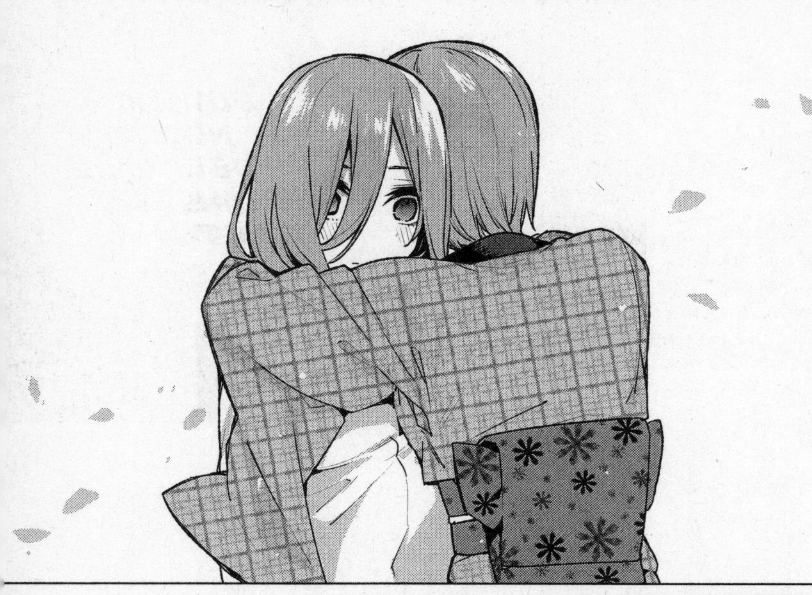

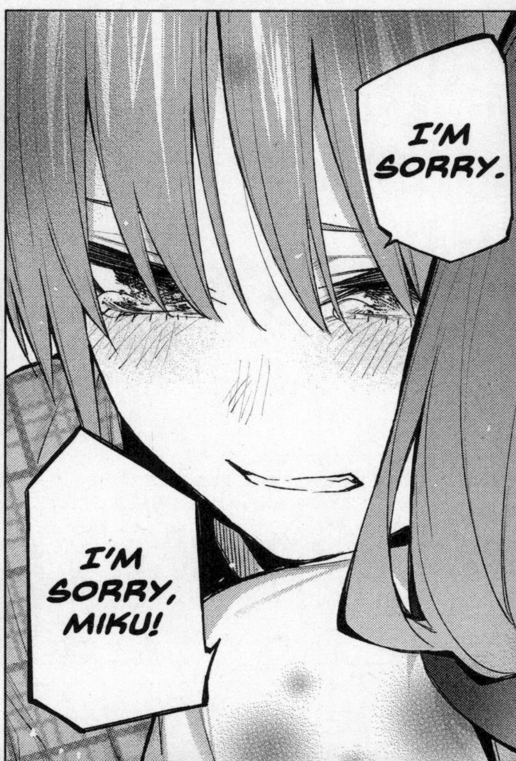
I'M SORRY.
I'M SORRY, MIKU!

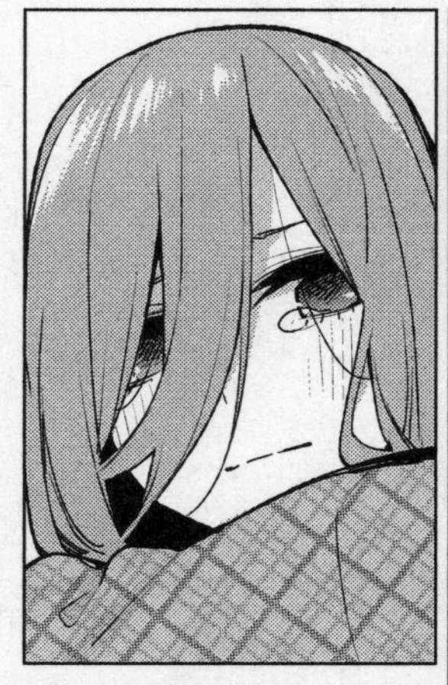

IT'S OKAY.

I NEVER KNEW LOVE HURT SO MUCH.

THANKS, ICHIKA.

OHHH! THIS IS WHERE YOU RAN OFF TO, UESUGI-KUN?
W-WE FINALLY FOUND YOU... HUH?

HMM? ALL THE NAKANOS'RE HERE! THIS IS MY CHANCE TO-
LET'S NOT BOTHER THEM NOW.
LET'S CHECK UT THE IGHTS, IST THE THREE OF US.

HURK!
GRAB

HOW ABOUT WE START WITH THE HAUNTED HOUSE?
AGAIN?!
AND WHY DON'T WE EXCHANGE CONTACT INFO, TOO?
THIS IS ALL RATHER SUDDEN.

WHATEVER IT IS THEY DID AND TALKED ABOUT...

...FROM THE TIME WE LEFT TO THE TIME EVERYONE MET BACK UP...

...IS KNOWN ONLY TO THE FIVE OF THEM.

Sign: (top) Historical Dramas
(bottom) House of Disguise

I GUESS I CAUSED SOME TROUBLE FOR YOU TOO, HUH?
SORRY.

THIS E COURSE... THE STUDIO TOUR...
I CHOSE IT AFTER CONSIDERING THE POSSIBILITY YOU WOULD EACH CHOOSE SEPARATE COURSES...

BECAUSE I ASSUMED THIS IS WHERE YOU'D COME, ICHIKA.

WH-WHY ME?
...AL-THOUGH THAT WAS BASED ONLY ON THE FACT THAT YOU'RE AN ACTRESS.

ER... WELL...
I WENT TOO FAR...
AND I DIDN'T LISTEN TO YOUR SIDE OF THINGS...
I FEEL PRETTY BAD ABOUT THAT.

I'LL SAY!

GLARING AT A GIRL LIKE THAT... HOW LOW CAN A GUY GET?
SORRY...
I WAS REALLY SAD.
SORRY...
OH, I'M JUST KIDDING.

IT WAS ALL A LIE.
HUH?!
"ALL"?

ALL
OF IT.

THANK YOU FOR RIDING WITH US TODAY.
WE WILL MOMENTARILY ARRIVE AT KYOTO STATION.
WHOOSH

WHAT DID SHE MEAN BY "ALL OF IT"?
DID YOU HEAR ABOUT THAT VOYEUR PHOTO COMMOTION, UESUGI-KUN?
SORRY. MY BAD.

...
I FIGURED IT WAS YOU.

HONESTLY, YOU SHOULD KNOW THERE'S A TIME AND A PLACE FOR EVERYTHING.
I GOT A LITTLE CARRIED AWAY.
SIGH.

WELL, NO HARM, NO FOUL.
I DID ASK YOU TO DO IT, AFTER ALL.
SKREEK
THE TOR-RENTIAL DOWNPOUR STOPPED.
HMM?
WE SEEM TO HAVE PICKED UP A FEW MORE PASSENGERS THAN WE ARRIVED WITH...
AND I'M SURE...
...THEY'LL BE STRONGER FOR HAVING WEATHERED THE STORM.

OKAY.
SAY CHEESE.

HERE.
GIVE THIS TO EVERY-ONE.

HUH?
WHAT IS IT?
PAYBACK FOR THE BIRTHDAY PRESENTS.

!
AN ALBUM...

I'M BROKE, SO THERE'S NO WAY I CAN BUY FIVE PRESENTS.
SO I MADE ONE.
I ENLISTED TAKEDA AND MAEDA TO HELP ME CREATE THIS RECORD OF YOU SISTERS' MEMORIES.

COME TO THINK OF IT...
SO MUCH HAP-PENED...
...THAT WE MAY HAVE FORGOTTEN TO TAKE A PHOTO TOGETHER...

THANK YOU, FUTARO-KUN.
I'LL SHOW THE OTHERS.
I FIGURED YOU WERE GOING TO PULL SOMETHING IN KYOTO, TOO...
W-
WELL, I DID TRY SOME-THING, BUT...YOU KNOW HOW IT IS...
ANYWAY...

RENA...
...I'M GRATEFUL TO YOU.

IF I HADN'T RUN INTO YOU THAT DAY, I MIGHT'VE BEEN ALONE FOREVER.
I HAVE YOU TO THANK FOR THE CURRENT ME.
MY FIRST TRIP TO KYOTO SINCE THAT ONE SIX YEARS AGO...ENDED BEFORE I KNEW IT...
...BUT I MADE THIS ALBUM BELIEVING IT WOULD LEAD TO GOOD MEMORIES IN THE FUTURE.

THANKS A LOT.
SHK
ITSUKI
!
SORRY FOR DOING THIS ON MY OWN.

BUT I THINK YOU SHOULD TELL HIM.
THAT THE GIRL HE MET SIX YEARS AGO...
...WAS YOU.

NO.

IT'S BETTER THIS WAY.

ONTINUED IN VOLUME 11!

WHAT IF SISTERS' WAR ~EVERYONE GOT ALONG

AHAHAHA!
THIS APP IS AMAZING, HUH?!
OUR FACES REALLY SWITCHED!
I WOULD LIKE TO TRY IT NEXT!
WHOA
THIS PAIRING IS TOO WILD!
IT LOOKS SO WRONG!
COME ON, STOP IT!
HUH?
IT'S HAVING TROUBLE IDENTIFYING OUR FACES...
PFFT!
DON'T SWAP THEM WHEN I'M NOT EXPECTING IT!
MY SIDES!

Staff Ueno Hino Cho Naito

Something's Wrong With Us

NATSUMI ANDO

The dark, psychological, sexy shojo series readers have been waiting for!

A spine-chilling and steamy romance between a Japanese sweets maker and the man who framed her mother for murder!

Following in her mother's footsteps, Nao became a traditional Japanese sweets maker, and with unparalleled artistry and a bright attitude, she gets an offer to work at a world-class confectionary company. But when she meets the young, handsome owner, she recognizes his cold stare...

THE SWEET SCENT OF LOVE IS IN THE AIR! FOR FANS OF OFFBEAT ROMANCES LIKE *WOTAKOI*

In an office romance, there's a fine line between sexy and awkward... and that line is where Asako — a woman who sweats copiously — meets Koutarou — a perfume developer who can't get enough of Asako's, er, scent. Don't miss a romcom manga like no other!

A Kodansha Comics Trade Paperback Original

Published in the United States by Kodansha Comics, an imprint of Kodansha USA Publishing, LLC, New York.

Publication rights for this English edition arranged through Kodansha Ltd., Tokyo.

First published in Japan in 2019 by Kodansha Ltd., Tokyo as *Gotoubun no hanayome*, volume 10.

ISBN 978-1-63236-996-3

Cover Design: Saya Takagi (RedRooster)

Printed in the United States of America.

www.kodanshacomics.com

9 8 7 6 5 4 3 2 1
Translation: Steven LeCroy
Lettering: Jan Lan Ivan Concepcion
Additional Layout: Belynda Ungurath
Editorial Assistance: YKS Services LLC/SKY Japan, INC.
Kodansha Comics edition cover design by Phil Balsman

Publisher: Kiichiro Sugawara
Vice president of marketing & publicity: Naho Yamada

Director of publishing services: Ben Applegate
Associate director of operations: Stephen Pakula
Publishing services managing editor: Noelle Webster
Assistant production manager: Emi Lotto, Angela Zurlo